To Timbuktu and Beyond
A MISSIONARY MEMOIR

David L. Marshall with Ted T. Cable

WESTBOW
PRESS
A DIVISION OF THOMAS NELSON

WestBow Press books may be ordered through booksellers or by contacting:

WestBow Press
A Division of Thomas Nelson
1663 Liberty Drive
Bloomington, IN 47403
www.westbowpress.com
1-(866) 928-1240

Because of the dynamic nature of the Internet, any Web addresses or links contained in this book may have changed since publication and may no longer be valid. The views expressed in this work are solely those of the author and do not necessarily reflect the views of the publisher, and the publisher hereby disclaims any responsibility for them.

Any people depicted in stock imagery provided by Thinkstock are models, and such images are being used for illustrative purposes only.

Certain stock imagery © Thinkstock.

ISBN: 978-1-4497-0808-5 (sc)
ISBN: 978-1-4497-0809-2 (hc)
ISBN: 978-1-4497-0807-8 (e)

Library of Congress Control Number: 2010940628

Printed in the United States of America

WestBow Press rev. date: 11/19/2010

Dedication

This book is dedicated to Elaine, my wonderful wife of over sixty two years, with whom I shared these experiences and many others; some very difficult, but most joyful, exciting and fun; and also to our three wonderful children each born on a different continent, but all having exciting and fun childhood's growing up in Timbuktu.

Contents

Dedication v
Foreword ix
Acknowledgements. xi
Preface xiii

Chapter 1. Childhood Challenges 1
Chapter 2. Commitments 5
Chapter 3. Off to Africa 27
Chapter 4. Arriving in Africa 45

PRE-TIMBUKTU. 53

Chapter 5. To Timbuktu 59
Chapter 6. Our Life in Timbuktu. 73
Chapter 7. Establishing Our Ministry 87
Chapter 8. First Furlough. 107
Chapter 9. Back Home in Timbuktu 115

TIMBUKTU. 125

Chapter 10. Building the Mission Station 137
Chapter 11. The Niger Gospel Boat 143
Chapter 12. The Bookstore Ministry 151
Chapter 13. Our Children's Education. 157
Chapter 14. Serving By Leading. 167

POST-TIMBUKTU 175

Chapter 15. Romania. 181
Chapter 16. Living Water Project. 193
Chapter 17. "Retirement" and Reflections 203

About the Authors 211

Foreword

I have a special place in my heart for great stories, particularly stories about people who have had an impact on my life. So, when I heard that Dave Marshall was chronicling his life journey I was delighted knowing that many would be blessed. Dave and Elaine are special people in many ways. At first meeting they seem thoughtful, quiet and unassuming. They are kind and gracious, down home sort of folk. They are the kind of people that you immediately feel you can trust and hope that they like you enough to let you into their friendship. And when they do you become aware that you are sharing life and ministry with 'a cut above' caliber people. I have had the pleasure of being their pastor, working with Dave on the board of Evangelical Baptist Missions when he was the president and have visited the field in Mali where they served as missionaries. Knowing them through the years has convinced me that their steady undaunted and strong commitment to Jesus and his cause is the real deal.

As you read through these pages you will be inspired by the evident hand of God in their lives. I've always felt that you can see God's hand in life best through the rear view mirror. Dave has graciously let us look in that mirror with him and with transparent candor has reflected on his struggles and successes as he has sought to live and work to advance the work of Christ. I like biographies because I am always challenged to greater heights of living and leadership as I see the strengths of the subject of the book in action. There is a magnetic dynamic about the stimulating reality of a life well lived that moves all of us forward and upward in our own lives. This book will do that for you.

I am proud to be known as Dave and Elaine Marshalls friend. I trust that the story of their lives will be as helpful to you as their friendship has been to me.

Joseph M. Stowell

President, Cornerstone University and *Strength for the Journey* web ministry, author of numerous books including *The Trouble with Jesus, Following Christ, Simply Jesus and You,* and *Radical Reliance* and former President of Moody Bible Institute

Acknowledgements

I want to thank the many people who have encouraged me to share with you the very special privilege God gave to Elaine and me to take the gospel to "The end of the earth" and preach to wonderful people of Timbuktu who we came to know and love. I would also like to thank my son-in-law Ted Cable for the hours of editing and coordinating with the publishers, Ron and Barb Pierre for their support of this book, and to Elaine for typing the manuscript. Finally, I would like to thank all of the individuals and churches who have shared in and supported our ministry over the past sixty years.

Preface

Many people encouraged me to write my memoirs. I have been hesitant, because I did not believe there was anything important to write about myself. I was a poor student as a child and even at a Bible school. When I first applied to be a missionary, I was turned down. What could I write about that is noteworthy? Then it occurred to me that my story is not about *me*; rather, it is about how the hand of Lord used me with all of my failures to His glory. Therefore, this book is not meant to be merely a history or a biography but a testimony. After more than sixty years of missionary service and seeing the hand of God work miracle after miracle, I feel an obligation to share with you what God has done and His mighty works that I witnessed over six wonderful decades of serving Him. I trust that through this book you will be encouraged in your service to God, whatever and wherever that might be.

Chapter 1.
Childhood Challenges

Train up a child in the way he should go: and when he is old he will not depart from it. Proverbs 22:6

I don't know whether my mother delivered me at Montgomery Hospital or at home at 1332 Markley Street in Norristown, Pennsylvania, but on March 14, 1928, I weighed in at an even ten pounds. I was the third son of James Earl and Emily S. (Furlong) Marshall. My older brothers were Gordon Kenneth and James Donald, and my younger brother was Frank Howard. The last three of us were born within three years and one day.

I assume that my folks were fairly well-to-do, or at least had a good line of credit, as they had nice furniture, and in 1929, my father bought a brand-new Pontiac sedan. They had a new beautiful home on the drawing board that was to be built on the corner of Markley and Brown streets. Brown Street ended at Markley, which had a quaint round pond with a fountain in the middle, shooting water into the air.

Down the center of Markley Street, trolley tracks connected Norristown with Allentown. At the terminus on Main Street, the Lehigh Valley Transit Company connected with the P & W (Philadelphia and Western), which was a bullet-shaped high-speed trolley that went to 69th Street in Philadelphia and from there connected to the city's elevated and subway system.

Our new home had a laundry chute that went from the second floor to the basement. In the basement, my mother had a mangler that she used to iron flat pieces, like sheets, towels, socks, and undershirts. My mother ironed everything until we all got married. Her daughters-in-law finally convinced her that you did not have to iron Turkish towels, underwear, and sheets. We had a wonderful maid, Mattie. We four boys kept her busy.

I was a mischievous kid, and by age four, I was already in trouble. I picked up a rock one day and placed it on the trolley tracks and then sat down on the terrace, patiently waiting for the next trolley to come to see if it would crush the stone. It didn't—but what it did was derail the trolley. After a couple of hours, a crane was brought to the rescue and lifted it back on the tracks, and it continued on its way. I don't remember the licking that I received, but it did the trick and I never did that again.

But I did do other things. When I was five years old, I was convinced I could show one of my brothers a new game. Our next-door neighbor had a two-car garage where the doors opened onto an alley. The doors had about forty glass windowpanes, and the alley was gravel. The game we played was to see who could break the most windows. We could not even count yet, and I don't remember who was winning when Mattie came around the corner and began to chase after us. We ran as hard as we could to a field about two long blocks away, and we lay down in the tall grass, but Mattie prevailed, and I think within a day or so, our bottoms were as dark as Mattie's. She did the right thing, and we never played that game again. Mattie was part of the family, and while she was the maid, my mother treated her like one of the family, and I'm sure she taught my mother many things as well.

In 1932, we all piled into the Pontiac to go to the Norris Theater to see Shirley Temple in *The Good Ship Lollypop.* That was the only time I ever remember my folks taking us to see the movies. If my memory serves me right, it was while we were at the movies that it began to rain so hard that it created a huge flood. Norristown has two creeks that run through it, Sawmill Run and Stony Creek, both of which empty into the Schuylkill River, which separates Norristown from Bridgeport. Stony Creek runs through Elmwood Park, on the north end of which was the zoo, which was well-populated with animals—bears, lions, tigers, geese, parrots, deer, and who knows what else. The park flooded that night, and all the animals escaped. A field just across Markley Street separated our house from the zoo. Fortunately, the field was much higher than the creek and the zoo, so we got a chance to see all the animals in the wild until they were captured and the water receded, when they were all put back behind bars in cages. By now I think I should have been put behind bars.

The Crash

I was not aware of the Depression until we had to move from our lovely home on Markley Street into a duplex on Pine and Roberts Street, directly across from the Rittenhouse Junior High School. I was too young to understand what was going on. Dad was out of work, and money was scarce. We had lost our home and now rented. With the house was a two-car garage, which stored the Pontiac and my grandfather Marshall's Studebaker. (I never knew my grandparents on my mother's side, as they both had died before I was one year old.) My dad tried his luck as a salesman. I don't know how he got money to buy the soap, string, cord, wire, and other household products he sold. Perhaps it was given to him on consignment.

Mattie was gone but remained a good friend. Her husband, Virgil Sims, was the custodian at the Norris Theater, and they kept the six of us supplied with the handkerchiefs that people would leave at the theater after wiping their eyes and noses from sad scenes. Mattie always made sure they were washed and ironed and perfectly clean. I can remember more than once our former maid sending us food.

To help put food on the table, we took in boarders. One was Miss Black, a schoolteacher who taught across the street. Another was my mother's nephew. He was a prominent magician and also taught magic and sold magic equipment in Philadelphia. His name was Andrew Furlong. One of his slickest tricks was that after he owed us for six months' room and board, he came downstairs to ask my mother for some clothesline, as he was practicing a new trick. Later that evening, he used the rope to lower his suitcases from his upstairs window, and he never returned again. He was thoughtful and left the rope.

I began first grade at Roosevelt Elementary School, also on Markley Street. First grade was only half a day. Before the school year ended, we moved again. This move took us to live with my grandparents at 203 Summit Street. I assume it was because my parents could not pay their rent. I continued walking a mile and half to Roosevelt School to finish out the school year.

Grandpop and Grandmom were courageous to take in a family of six. Grandpop had owned a textile or wool mill in Norristown, but I assume he lost it in the early years of the Depression. They previously had a home in Fairview Village where he raised rabbits in a one hundred-foot-long cage. But because of a serious asthmatic condition and allergies to the rabbit fur, he had to give it up and move back to town. It was there that they were invaded by four boys ages six to twelve.

To relieve his asthma, Grandpop sat on the front porch with a pot of what looked like sulfur. He would burn it with his face bent down so he could breathe the yellow smoke coming from the pot. The ceiling over the covered porch was yellow from the smoke. Alongside the pot was the spittoon, as coughing went along with the disease. It was horrible listening to him coughing and gasping for breath. Shortly thereafter he succumbed to the illness and he died. This was my first experience with death and in the funeral home looking on a corpse I was horrified when I saw my father bend over the casket and kiss my granddad goodbye. I was also trying to make the connection between the undertaker and his name which was Homer Dunaway. Being very young I believe, only seven, I never heard anyone ever mention whether or not he was a believer although I do have assurance that my grandmother who lived to be ninety-three had trusted Christ as her Savior. At age seven death was a scary thing to me, but as a believing adult, I would learn not to fear death even as I came close to dying.

Chapter 2.
Commitments

Commit thy way unto the Lord; trust also in him; and he shall bring it to pass. Psalms 37:5

Conversion

Bob and Dick DeWees lived down the street and around the corner from us. They were twins whose mother died in childbirth. An uncle and aunt took them in and raised them the best they could, but the boys had such a bad reputation that we were not supposed to hang out with them. I'm not sure if the bad influence was them or me. During the summer of 1936, the twins arrived at our door with an invitation to go with them to a vacation Bible school. We were encouraged to go with the "bad boys" to church. We were Methodist, but the Bible school was being held at the Bible Testimony Church, and on the marquee it said, "Nondenominational, Independent, Fundamental." We had no idea what all that meant but eventually would find out.

We memorized Bible verses and had handwork, story time, snacks, playtime, and singing. On the last Friday, our parents were invited to come in the evening for our closing exercises. I attended, along with my brothers, Gordon and Frank. Don was home with a badly infected hand from a stab wound with a cuticle knife that he had inflicted upon himself while carving a piece of wood. Dad went to the closing exercises, while Mom took care of Don. He was impressed with all we had learned and with the people. The impression was so strong that our family began attending the church. Our pastor was Ben Male, a student at Westminster Seminary. He and his wife, Mary, had a great love for people. Pastor had a big LaSalle roadster, and at one time they had eighteen kids in it going to a special meeting. The church met in a small, former Quaker meeting house. Pastor Male was from Colorado, and to us kids, he was a cowboy just off of the ranch. We could imagine where he came from because five days a week we listened to the radio between five and six o'clock to fifteen minutes of *Tom Mix, The Lone Ranger, Terry and the Pirates,* and *Jack Armstrong,* "The All-American Boy." These radio dramatizations held us spellbound and exercised our imaginations far more than television would ever do.

At church, we had special evangelistic meetings and Bible conferences. They would run from Sunday through Sunday and occasionally for two weeks. The League of Nations from Practical Bible Training School in Binghamton, New York, visited the church. This student group represented many different countries, with the students dressed in native garb. I can still visualize the Dutch girl and Abou Sabadas Nelson from India. He told a story about arriving in New York from India and going to the station to go to Chicago. He said the agent told him he would have to go via Buffalo and he responded that he did not want to go by buffalo but by train. He stayed overnight with us, and we had a ball entertaining this Indian student.

Sunday became a day we looked forward to as we went to Sunday school, followed by church and again church that evening. We lived a couple miles from the church. We did not have a car, so we walked and always hoped we were going on the same street that Mr. and Mrs. Mayberry drove on. They lived just a few doors from the twins, and it was a treat when they would stop and offer us a ride.

During the course of a year, Mother, Dad, and us four boys all trusted Christ as our Savior. I vividly remember one Sunday night going to bed and laying there thinking as a nine-year-old boy about my sin. No one had to convince me that I was a sinner. I knew it, and so did everyone else. By now I had memorized John 1:1–12, John 3:16, Romans 3:23, Romans 6:23, and others. Through the hearing of the preaching of the word of God and the verses I had memorized, I remember making the decision to crawl out of bed and kneel down, asking God's forgiveness. My bedroom was on the third floor in a partially finished attic. I don't remember the date, but I do remember that my burden of sin was lifted and Christ took that load from me. Many, many times I've had to go back and confess sin in my life, but He has always been faithful to forgive and cleanse me from *all* unrighteousness.

My dad later became the church janitor, earning a couple dollars a week. One Sunday night, a huge man who weighed more than three hundred pounds (everyone called him "Tiny") offered to drive my mother and brothers home. He was a bachelor and took care of his elderly mother, who lived near us. Dad closed up the church and walked home, and when he opened the front door, Mom said, "Where's David?"

"I thought he was with you," replied Dad.

"No, I left him with you!"

So, Dad made the long walk back to the church, where he found me asleep on the pew. That was a relief both for him and for me.

On the front wall behind the pulpit was a large sign painted in the shape of a scroll. On it was Isaiah 55:11, "My word shall not return unto me void." Truly, it did accomplish its purpose in the hearts and lives of the Marshalls. Ben Male completed his seminary work at Westminster and returned to Colorado, but not before the orthodox Presbyterian baptized by immersion my oldest brother, Gordon. Our church didn't have a baptismal pool, so we went to an old country church. I don't remember whether it had a pool or whether it was done in a nearby creek. Some problems apparently developed at the church after the Males left, and our family began going across the river to Bridgeport Baptist Church. On Easter Sunday 1940, Mom and Dad, along with Don, Frank, and I, were baptized and became members of the church. That same day, Elaine Beswick was baptized. Elaine Beswick would become Elaine Marshall eight years later. Our pastor, William Francis, was a faithful servant. I never saw Pastor Francis after he resigned to take another pastorate, but we did receive a letter from him after he turned one hundred years old, and he still had excellent handwriting.

Companionship

Our church was located in an industrial section of Bridgeport, directly across the street from the Summaril Tubing Company where my father worked during World War II. They manufactured hypodermic needles as well as steel tubing, and throughout the war, they worked seven days a week and twenty-four hours a day.

I met Elaine at Happy Hour in 1940. No, not *that* kind of happy hour! We were both twelve years old. Happy Hour was a Bible club that Pastor Francis had every Friday afternoon after school. I remember being outside the church and writing with a pencil on a Ping-Pong ball, "I love you" and giving it to a girl named Maude Hess to give to Elaine. I was so shy that I don't think I even watched her expression. Toward the end of the school year, I wanted to ask her for a date. I was too timid to ask her at church but got courage to call her on the phone.

I said, "Hi, Elaine, our high school is putting on a circus in our gym, and I was wondering if you would like to go with me."

There was a brief pause and then an, "Okay." We decided she could come from Bridgeport on the bus to Main and Swede streets in Norristown, where I would meet her. She would get a transfer, and I would board the bus with her to the closest bus stop near Norristown High School, which would be Powell and Brown. That would leave us about four and a half blocks to walk together. What I did not expect was that she would bring her girlfriend, Maude Hess, with her. It was a rainy, cold spring day. After the performance, we walked back to the bus stop, where I put the girls back on the bus and said good-bye. What a relief my first date was over! There were no hugs or kisses, but it was a start. The next few years brought a couple of more dates. Once we went to Riverview Beach in Delaware. We would take the high-speed trolley from Bridgeport to Sixty-ninth Street in Philadelphia and then the "el" and subway to Market Street where we would board the Wilson Line, a riverboat that ran up and down the Delaware River. It left near the Ben Franklin Bridge, and it was a scenic ride past the navy yard at the mouth of the Schuylkill River. We would pass the Scott Paper Company in Chester, the oil refinery in Marcus Hook, oil tankers discharging crude oil, ships navigating the river, and tug boats dashing here and there. On board you could treat your girlfriend to a popsicle, a coke, a hot dog, or cracker-jacks, any one for a nickel or all for a quarter. But the boat's slot machines (one-armed bandits) could rob you of your penny or nickel. Riverview Park featured many rides, including a Ferris wheel, bumper cars, the spook house, and a swimming pool. These dates usually terminated with a peck on the cheek.

When needing money for a date, we never thought of asking our parents for it but rather found ways to earn a buck or two. When I was twelve years old, I was selling and delivering *The Ladies Home Journal, The Saturday Evening Post,* and other magazines. I went door to door selling chocolate candy like Easter eggs and other fine chocolates that were homemade in the basement of a German immigrant who lived on Powell Street. We would buy a box of 120 pieces for one dollar and sell them for a penny a piece. I'd make twenty cents on a box if I didn't eat any of them. Another way to earn "date money" was selling Christmas cards and all-occasion cards. I used to get Christmas cards from the General

Card Company in Chicago and the all-occasion cards from the Sunshine Line. We could get Christmas cards with names printed on them for fifty cards for a dollar, with envelopes. The Scripture cards from the Sunshine Line sold twenty-four for a dollar. We made 25 to 50 percent on a box of cards. Another money-maker was finding old pop bottles. Deposits were five cents on a quart bottle and two cents on a small bottle. A Coke, Pepsi, or 7-UP would cost a nickel, plus a two-cent deposit. Many people threw their empty bottles away rather than taking them back to the store for a refund. Coke came in a six-fluid-ounce bottle. The Pepsi Company bottle was twelve ounces. They had a jingle they played on the radio. *"Pepsi Cola hits the spot. Twelve full ounces, that's a lot. Twice as much for a nickel too. Pepsi Cola is the drink for you!"*

When I turned fifteen years old, I was fortunate to be able to go away to a boarding school near Media, Pennsylvania, The Williamson Free School of Mechanical Trades. This was a prestigious school for underprivileged kids. We had academic classes half a day and studied a trade for a half day five days a week. The students were divided according to trades, such as painting and interior decorating, machinist, carpentry, power plant, and masonry. I was in the masonry division (which was providential, as these skills would be essential later). This was my tenth year of school, and I could go home for a weekend about once a month. On weekends, we had jobs to do, such as rake leaves, shovel snow, unload coal cars, and fill an old dump truck with coal and haul it to the power plant and a lot of odd jobs. At the Williamson School each year, a tailor from one of the Wanamaker Stores in Philadelphia would come out and measure us and provide us with new clothes each year. On Sunday, my brother and I wore these clothes to the First Baptist Church of Media.

World War II was in progress, and my oldest brother got a job at the Sun Oil Company after graduating high school. It was obvious that he would be drafted into the army, so he enlisted into the army air corps, where he became a pilot of a B-17. He ended up flying fifty missions out of Foggia, Italy, but on his fourteenth mission, he was hit by flak. A piece of shrapnel tore into his head. When he regained consciousness, he had to take control of his plane, as the co-pilot was beside himself with the sight of all the blood. He completed his mission and returned to his base, and after a couple of weeks in the base hospital, he was back in the air. Gordon was awarded the Distinguished Flying Cross, a Purple Heart, and two Air Medals.

During my summer vacation in 1944, I worked as an apprentice bricklayer for Bob Thompson, a bricklaying contractor from Phoenixville, Pennsylvania. On a Wednesday evening, I was attending prayer meeting, and we had a special speaker, a missionary who worked in the Kentucky mountains with The Kentucky Mountain Mission. My heart was challenged that evening, and I dedicated my life for missionary service. I was the only young person at church that evening, as Elaine and the other young people had gone to Keswick Bible Conference for the week. The following Sunday night, the pastor asked if anyone wanted to share a testimony. One after one, the young people, including Elaine and my brother Frank, shared how God had challenged them at camp with missions and that they had dedicated their lives to the Lord to go anywhere God would lead them. The work that God had done in their hearts, He had also done in my heart.

I was a poor student, and after a couple months back at Williamson, I quit and went back to Norristown High School. I was put into the vocational course, where again I had shop each afternoon, but now it was plumbing and sheet metal. That went okay, except for my English classes. My English teacher was a retired army colonel and ran the English class like the army. I got to the point where I felt lost in his class with no hope. I was totally frustrated! He had assigned a written book report, and it was due on Friday. I was a poor reader, and when I took a book in hand and began to read, my mind was somewhere else. He had a rule that if your book report was not in on the due date, the following week you would owe him two book reports, and if you missed that one, then you would owe four and so on. It got to the point where I owed him sixty-four reports! I would never make it. My escape would be that the next week I would turn seventeen, and I would be old enough to join the navy. My brother Don had also quit Williamson and had been accepted as a cadet in the merchant marine academy. On March 14, 1945, I skipped school, went to Philadelphia, and joined the navy.

Country

The recruiters sent me home and told me they would notify me where to report for active duty. A couple of weeks later, I received vouchers for train tickets and orders to report to Bainbridge, Maryland, on May 1 to begin boot camp.

When we arrived at Bainbridge, we were ordered to take all our clothes off, and we were issued two sets of white uniforms, two sets of blue uniforms, one set of dress uniforms, socks, skivvies, hats, and two pairs of shoes (one dress and one high-top work). We were also issued a mattress and mattress cover and two dog tags. The next morning in the mess hall, I happily discovered a lot of food that was hard to find back home. At home food and products such as soap, gasoline, and tires were rationed and scarce.

That morning in the chow line, they served a half a grapefruit, which they dipped in sugar. The wet juice of the grapefruit sucked up the sugar like a sponge. After breakfast, we had our physicals, and they took blood and urine samples. Later that day, I was informed that I needed to have another physical the next day, as my sugar was too high. I would be sent home if my sugar was high again. That scared me, as the last place I wanted to go was home, as they had just cut off all of my hair and I looked like an idiot! I avoided any desert or sugar the rest of the day and also had no sugared grapefruit for breakfast. Fortunately, that did the trick, and I passed. I was six-foot-two and a skinny 150 pounds. I tried my best to put on some weight by going through the mess hall twice every meal, but to no avail. With the exercises we would do, I burned off calories faster than I put them on, although I don't think any of us knew what calories were back in those days. It seemed when we had gym sessions, I was always matched against the biggest guy in our company. Those big brutes would pin me to the mat so fast I didn't know what happened, and they thought they were Charles Atlas.

Three days into boot camp came VE day, and the war in Europe was over. I wasn't sure if VE day was Victory in Europe or victory for Eisenhower. Boot camp lasted eight weeks, and then we were given seven days of leave. We were given our first promotion after boot camp, and we advanced from apprentice seaman to seaman second class. That meant a pay raise from $65 to $72 a month. I went home, and my brother Gordon was home from Italy, and I helped him drive his car from Norristown to Columbus, Ohio, where he was stationed. He promised to get me on an air force plane back to Philadelphia. That did not happen, so I hitchhiked back home and back to my base in Bainbridge, Maryland.

Upon arriving, I received orders to go to the USS *Portsmouth* CL102, which was anchored in Norfolk, Virginia. I had my sea bag with my mattress tied over the top, with the ends lashed down the two sides. I was met at the pier by some sober and some not-so-sober sailors. It was pitch dark, as we were still at war with Japan. We climbed into a motor launch, and after about a half an hour in the dark, we pulled up alongside of our ship. It was now after midnight, and I was bushed, as I had traveled almost nonstop from Columbus to Norfolk. I struggled with the weight of my sea bag getting up the gangway. Saluting the "officer of the day" at the top was a challenge, as I couldn't even see the guy. He ordered a seaman who was standing nearby to show me to my bunk. He had a small flashlight that was shining on his highly polished shoes as he walked along the teak deck, which had been painted battleship blue. We came to a hatch, and after going through sets of heavy canvas curtains, which blocked any light from escaping up on the top deck, we went down a ladder to the fifth division. I was shown my bunk, and then my escort disappeared. My bunk was the third one up, just under the fourth one. We were about fifty men sleeping in this compartment, which was just forward of the hangar deck, which housed three seaplanes.

The USS *Portsmouth* (CL102) had just been commissioned a week earlier, and all of the crew members who were on board at that time were given a certificate stating that they were "plank owners" of the *Portsmouth*. I felt cheated!

The next couple of days were spent loading ammunition on the ship. Our main batteries were six-inch guns with three per turret and four turrets. There were the five-inch guns, six turrets each with two guns. There also were six or eight turrets of forty mm machine guns each with four guns. It was a long day loading ammunition. Ammo was brought to the ship on barges and loaded from the barges onto our decks with floating cranes and a crane on the ship. The five- and six-inch projectiles were heavy, plus the powder kegs were equally as heavy. Each projectile required a powder keg. Powder kegs also were used to catapult our airplanes off of the ship.

Our destination was Guantanamo Bay, Cuba, where we would spend a couple of months on a shakedown cruise testing everything—engines, guns, radar, speed, towing ability, and practicing passing fuel lines and a sick or wounded sailors from one ship to the other. Our ship had four engines and four screws. Our cruising speed was fifteen knots, and full speed was twenty knots. Our maximum speed was about twenty-eight knots, but either the screws or shaft were not balanced enough, so at that speed, the whole back end of ship would vibrate.

While towing a heavy cruiser, the USS *Little Rock,* the cable broke and wound around one of the screws. The engines were shut down while two divers went overboard to unwrap the cable. The ship was surrounded by sharks that had been attracted by garbage ejected from the galley. Marines with rifles stood on the fantail shooting at the sharks that were trying to attack the live human bait. Our divers finally gave up, and we went to a dry dock in San Juan, Puerto Rico, to unwind the cable.

My battle station was on the forty-millimeter quads loading ammunition clips into the guns. We were next to the five-inch guns, which were deafening when they fired. The concussion nearly knocked me over. Tug boats would pull moving targets, at which our big guns would fire. Sometimes these were over the horizon, so you were dependent upon your radar to give you accurate distances and positions, trusting you were firing on the target and not the tug. At times, we would bombard a small, uninhabited island. Sometimes they would launch radio-controlled drones to simulate an air attack. Other times real planes would appear, towing sleeves behind them. Our job was to shoot at the sleeve and not the plane. It was not unusual for a pilot to disappear and quit when our fire got too close for comfort. About every fifth or sixth machine gun shell had a tracer on it. so you could see it as it went through the air. These exercises lasted six months.

During this time, I was sent away to school for two weeks to become an operator of a "director" for our quad forty-millimeter machine guns. A "director" was a machine with an instrument in it that was connected to radar. As I would capture my target in the viewer, I had to get the crosshairs in a floating bubble and then fire, keeping the crosshairs on that little bubble. The "director" calculated the speed of the target as well as the direction, and supposedly our projectiles would meet the target in the air. This was dependent on crew members below deck who made calculations from the radar and made the necessary adjustments electronically to my "director." Our radar antenna was mounted on our turret with four guns. My job was pretty exciting for a seventeen-year-old. After about six months of testing our guns with the radar equipment, we were ordered to Philadelphia. We were told there were problems between Italy and Yugoslavia over the border city of Trieste and that we would be sailing to the Adriatic Sea in case violence erupted between the two countries. Reserves like me made up most of our crew. We were to be discharged within the next month, but we were encouraged to extend our enlistment for a few months. I had never been to Europe, so I decided to reenlist. I was given a seventy-two-hour pass and went home to spend time with family and in particular to see Elaine.

As we left Philly and started down the Delaware River, I learned that we were not going to Italy but instead were headed for Africa. My watch on ship was on the bridge, and my job was that of helmsmen or standing at the engine telegraph controlling the speed of the ship. At the helm, I was given the course to steer by the officer of the day and the speed of the four engines. Our standard speed was fifteen knots or about twenty miles per hour. On this trip we were going at full speed—twenty knots.

When we left Philadelphia, we took on a marine band and an admiral, as this was a goodwill tour and we would host dignitaries from the countries where we would put into port. Our first port of call in Africa was Cape Town, South Africa. We spent eight days there. I got the surprise of my life. My conception of Africa was jungle, wild animals, and natives living in grass huts. Was I surprised! I had never seen anything in America more modern and beautiful than Cape Town, with Table Top Mountain in the background. Friendly people arranged sightseeing tours and many activities for us. They chauffeured us in their private cars and treated us royally. Apartheid was very evident, and segregation was obvious. Signs were very apparent: "Whites Only," "Colored Only," and Blacks Only." I felt sorry for the steward mates on our ship, not realizing that most of them were already accustomed to segregation. Where I grew up, there was no segregation, and some of my best friends were black. I sat next to blacks in school, on the bus, and on the train and used the same restrooms. I had nothing but respect for my black friends. My friend, Walter Campbell, used to tell me about his "white father," who I later found out was the Episcopalian priest at the mission church on Green St. In Junior High. Thomas Griffin, a black boy who was a straight-A student, made this white boy look awfully dumb. I admired him and his family, who obviously encouraged his achievement and were proud of his report card, which was so different than mine. The racism experienced in Cape Town was disturbing and unsettling.

Our next port of call was Lagos, Nigeria, a British colony. This was what I envisioned Africa to be. There was no dock, so we anchored out in a large lagoon that seemed to be surrounded by jungle. We spent three days there. I remember dugout canoes coming out and surrounding our ship. It was like a floating market, each with two or three people selling carvings, leather goods, ivory, grass-woven mats, and snake skins. I bought a leopard skin and wrote a letter to my parents telling them that I bought a "leper" skin. In my next letter from home, I was given a spelling lesson. The merchants were also terrific divers. They begged us to throw coins into the water, and they would dive out of the dugout and retrieve it while it was going to the bottom. They made a lot of money with their diving skills. Later you could buy the coins back in the form of jewelry.

The next stop was Freetown, Sierra Leone, another British colony. En route to Freetown, I had to take my leopard skin and throw it overboard. The hide had not been tanned or cured. It began to ferment and stink in my small locker. It was putrid, and I guess it really smelled like a leper skin.

Freetown had a beautiful beach, and I can remember going swimming on the beach. I had my mother's old Kodak box camera, and I inscribed in large letters in the sand "ELAINE" and took a picture of it so Elaine would know I was thinking about her. Little did I realize that nearly ten years later, I would be back on the very same beach with Elaine and our three children.

From Sierra Leone, we back tracked to Monrovia, Liberia. We were there over fourth of July, 1946. There was no dock, and we anchored at sea quite a distance from the shore. We had a couple of motor launches on our ship, along with the captain's gig. The sea was quite rough, and on one of the trips to shore, the captain's gig sank. There was no loss of life, but we left the gig on the ocean floor.

Independence Day required us to have a parade. It was the rainy season, and it was drizzling. Monrovia had no paved streets, just lots of mud and puddles. We were all dressed in our white uniforms. We had thirteen hundred sailors on the ship, and two-thirds of us were in the parade. We started out with white uniforms, but we returned with brown uniforms. Liberia was an independent country and was never colonized. They did have foreign companies there exploiting them, as the country was rich in iron ore and rubber. These companies did not invest much in development of roads, power, water, agriculture, and transportation infrastructure. President Tubman, on a visit to Mali in the 1960s, in a speech he gave in Timbuktu said, "Liberia did not have the blessing of being colonized." This was after he had toured several former French colonies in West Africa, which had some paved roads, telephone, telegraph, a postal system, riverboats, factories, power stations, and schools. Although rural areas in most former colonies were still undeveloped, the cities had basic improvements, including air service.

From Liberia, we sailed to Dakar, Senegal, which was the political capital for nine French West African Colonies. They had an excellent harbor, with docks and a railroad that connected Dakar with Bamako, the capital of the French Sudan (now Mali). It was the seat of the governor general, who was over nine other governors in each of the colonies. The American consulate in Dakar was under the American ambassador in

Paris. Dakar had been an important base during the war, and they built an airfield. There were still U. S. air corps personnel based there, along with some aircraft, including several B17s. After several days in Dakar, we sailed to the Cape Verde Islands three hundred miles directly west of Dakar. I remember being at the helm on the bridge when the B17s began crossing over the bow of our ship and returning over the stern. They were actually so low that ocean water rippled from the air of their propellers. The captain ordered that our crane on the back of the ship be lowered, as he was afraid they might clip it. The pilots were having fun, but the captain was having a fit!

At Portugal's Cape Verde Islands, there were no docks, so we anchored in a bay. The water was so clear you could see the ship's screws. One of our crew baited a grappling hook with a piece of raw meat and threw it overboard. Within minutes, we were surrounded by sharks. A large shark bit into the grappling hook and got it caught in his mouth. A harpoon was lanced into its tail, and it was drug up the side and onto the deck. While several seamen stretched it out, one of the men took a long knife and punctured it several times, while another jammed a fire hose nozzle into its mouth while blood poured over the deck and down the side of the ship. As the blood ran into the sea, it drew dozens of sharks. That night we had shark steak for supper.

Our next stop was the beautiful port of Casablanca, Morocco. This French protectorate had gorgeous, palm-lined boulevards with restaurants and fancy shops. The Americans still maintained a base there, and there were still German prisoners of war who were working in the mess hall. Those of us visiting the base were invited to chow, which was very good. I bought a small silver sword for Elaine as a lapel pin. The Moroccans had many good silver and goldsmiths. Expended gun shells provided brass from which they made ornate round serving trays, each with Moorish designs hammered into them.

Before arriving at Casablanca, we fitted our ship with outrigger cables that extended out on both sides of the ship. For the next few weeks, we received an increase in pay because we were sailing in hazardous waters that had many mines laid during the war. We entered into the Mediterranean Sea, passing by the heavily fortified Rock of Gibraltar. We continued east, arriving at Naples, Italy. Our dock was a sunken ship that had turned over on its side. When we went ashore, we walked on the side of the ship, which had a row of stanchions welded on it, from which a rope was attached as a railing. That evening, I went in town for spaghetti. I was disappointed, as it did not compare with the spaghetti of Jenny and Lucy DeMenos, my next-door neighbors on Chain Street in Norristown. The next day, we toured Pompeii, which was being excavated from being buried by the volcano of Mt. Vesuvius. We learned that Pompeii was a wicked and sinful city. Was Pompeii's destruction a result of God's judgment?

Leaving Naples, we made a brief stop at Palermo on the Italian island of Sicily. We just stopped long enough to pick up a body. I do not know who it was. All I know is that it was put into cold storage for the rest of our trip. Our tour was almost complete, with just one more stop in the Azores Islands, a group of impoverished islands belonging to Portugal. While there, I purchased a golden tablecloth for my mother. Our next stop was the good ole United States. Within a day or two of arriving in New Haven, Connecticut, I received orders and a train ticket to Bainbridge, Maryland, where I received my honorable discharge and a train ticket to Norristown, Pennsylvania. My monthly pay was $105.00 per month, plus all the food I could eat, and my bunk on the ship. I got my last paycheck, plus $300 "mustering-out pay."

The *hand of the Lord* allowed me to visit six African countries and began to burden my heart for that continent.

Courtship and Calling

I used my $300 separation pay to buy a Hudson from a used car dealer in Conshohocken, about five miles from Norristown. Little did I know that it would only run one month. I found that the engine was not for my car but had been jerry rigged and put into my car. Before the car died, I called Elaine and asked about a date. I was still wearing my uniform when I picked her up. We had a nice time at Willow Grove amusement park.

Elaine had graduated from high school and worked as a telephone operator with the Bell Telephone Company in Norristown. This was before the direct dialing, and every call went through an operator. When you took the receiver off the hook, the operator would say, "Number, please." After you told her the number, the operator would take one of many cables with plugs on them and would somehow get you plugged into the right number. For someone just out of high school, she was making good money, about $25 a week.

Soon after I was discharged, I called Bob Thompson, the brick-laying contractor in Phoenixville who I had worked for before going in the navy. He took me on as an apprentice bricklayer.

Elaine was content with her job and liked the money. But while walking down the hill from Heavenerville to church on Sunday morning with her brother, Wilbur (home on summer vacation from the Moody Bible Institute), he said to Elaine, "I thought you were going to go to Bible school." That was all it took, just a nudge from Wilbur, to bring her thoughts back to the decision she had made at Keswick Bible Conference when she had dedicated her life for missionary service. On Monday, she resigned from her job, and within a couple days, she was enrolled at the Bible Institute of Pennsylvania. I too had enrolled in the night school there.

At the end of my first trimester, I quit my bricklaying job and enrolled in the day school program and lived at the school. I had the navy benefits that entitled me to schooling, books, and pay. Later I lived at home and commuted each day. Elaine was commuting, and it would give me time with her. One spring day, we decided to walk home from school. We made the trek of eighteen miles in about six hours, mostly taking River Road as it followed the Schuylkill River. We passed through Manayunk, Swedeland, and then to Bridgeport. We enjoyed the time together, but the next day we had sore legs.

During our second year at school, around Thanksgiving time, I popped the question to Elaine, "Will you marry me?" She answered yes with a kiss. I worked hard selling Christmas and greetings cards and saved what I thought was enough money to buy an engagement ring. My mother went with me to Rogers Jewelry Store on DeKalb Street in Norristown to help me pick it out. It wasn't much of a rock, just a pebble, but it has lasted over sixty years. Since then, we have added a couple more "pebbles" to the original, including the diamond from my grandfather's ring.

The Spurr family spoke and sang at a Bible school chapel period. They served on the staff at a church located at Broad and Master streets in Philadelphia and were involved with youth rallies every Saturday night. At the end of the chapel, Vernon, the father, invited me to come on staff as camp counselor at Youth Bible Congress (YBC).

In June, I rode in the back of the Spurrs' U-haul truck for the three hundred-mile trip to the camp in Perth, just north of Amsterdam, New York. I had a great summer living in the boys' dorm. Elaine's brother, Wilbur, was married that summer to Lorraine Vielhauer. He was invited to be a speaker at the camp, so Wilbur had his honeymoon at YBC as the speaker during the first week of his marriage.

At the end of summer, I returned home to King Manor, a suburb of Bridgeport, and started back to Bible school. Elaine and I made our wedding plans for the week after graduation on June 12, 1948. The Bible Institute of Pennsylvania was a two-year program. At graduation time, I had only completed a year and two-thirds, so I was given a "night school" diploma.

Our wedding was simple but nice. Elaine and I asked Theron and Thurlow Spurr to play the wedding march on their trumpets. They were in high school but were excellent players. They brought with them their music teacher from the Broadalbin School, a delightful elderly gentleman of Scottish descent with a pleasing accent. When the trumpets sounded and the march began, I looked up to see my beautiful bride coming down the aisle. She was gorgeous holding onto her father George's arm. We were surrounded by Elaine's maid of honor, her sister, Melba, my best man, Henry Henning, and the preacher, Elwood Bauers. Walter Laird, a blind friend, was the soloist. We had no money, so there was no photographer and only one basket of flowers but many friends. After the wedding ceremony, we had a reception at the Beswicks' home just up the street from the church.

The Lord provided enough monetary gifts to enable us to have a four-day honeymoon. Elaine's father loaned us his car, and after an hour at the reception, we took off, not knowing where we were going except to be heading toward the Pocono Mountains. Near Strasburg, we found some cabins with a vacancy. The price was between three and five dollars per night. We just stayed one night and then headed to Williamsport to visit my cousin Anne Butt and her husband, Mark, as well as my aunt, Ollie Furlong, my mother's sister-in-law. We spent Sunday night there and on Monday headed toward Arlington, Virginia, where my brother James (Donald) and his wife, Isabel, were living. On Monday evening, we stopped in Maryland and ate at a restaurant. We ordered fresh ham for supper. We were surprised when they served us white pork meat, as we thought ham should be pink. We spent Tuesday with Don and Isabel and headed home on Wednesday.

The first few days home were busy. The week before the wedding, Earl Kutz, a general contractor and a member of our church, had given me scaffold boards, some asphalt shingles, and two metal windows. The father of an usher in our wedding offered to saw the planks into two-by-fours. Earl loaned us his dump truck, which we loaded with the two-by-fours, shingles, windows, a door, an old toilet, and a big old sink. We arrived at

YBC in time for a banquet in our honor. Elaine wore her wedding dress. The pictures taken of us were our only wedding pictures taken seven days after the wedding.

With the donated materials, I quickly framed our twelve-by-twelve-foot cabin, including a small bathroom with no tub or shower, just a toilet and sink. It was big enough for a three-quarter-size bed and a dresser but not for a chair. The cabin sat on cement blocks on a hill about seventy-five feet from the boys' dorm. It was never finished off inside, just studs and rafters, but it served as home the first few months of our married life.

During that summer, we met Joe McCaba, a speaker at the camp. Joe was the founder of African Christian Missions, headquartered in Patterson, New Jersey. He had been a missionary in Nigeria with Sudan Interior Mission. His wife, Margaret Price, had been the secretary to Mr. Gregg, the inventor of the Gregg shorthand system. Together they founded the mission and established work in Niamey in the Niger colony of French West Africa.

Through Joe's ministry, God gave us a burden for the Muslims of West Africa. Joe had a way of grabbing your heart and squeezing it until you yielded to God. He was a unique Bible teacher, and being Syrian, he spoke fluent Arabic, as well as French, Hausa, and Zarma.

After that summer at YBC, we returned to Norristown, where we rented a room in a rooming house on Jacoby Street that belonged to the owner of Swap with Pop, a used furniture store on Main Street. The room had an ice box and a two-burner electric hot plate. The bathroom was down the hall and used by the half dozen or so people who rented rooms. While living there, Elaine took typing courses at the high school. One day Elaine had an upset stomach, and I went to the drug store to buy Pepto-Bismol. It didn't work. I had never heard of morning sickness, but it wasn't long before we both learned what caused this sickness. We found a larger unfurnished two-room apartment on West Elm Street. The bathroom again was shared by the family—not convenient for an expectant mother. Elaine's doctor was Dr. Seasongood. In those days you bought yellow and afterward you could go blue or pink, which ever was appropriate. On Sunday May 1, 1949, at about 5:00 PM, I learned that I was the father of David Lane Marshall Jr., and so blue would be appropriate. Elaine stayed in the hospital for eight or nine days, including Mother's Day, because our doctor was Jewish and had to wait until the eighth day to do the circumcision.

Later in 1949, we applied to Africa Christian Missions. We needed to go to Patterson to meet with the mission board, so we borrowed my father-in-law's car. We had enough money for gasoline to get to Patterson but knew that the Lord would in His own way meet our need to get us home. The mission office was in the old Stam home. John Stam and his wife Betty had been missionaries in China and had been beheaded by the communists several years earlier.

We met with the board at 7:00 PM. They were godly, elderly men. Before the evening was over, they told us that they rejected our applications because we were too young. We were greatly disappointed. It would be hard to explain to family and friends. As we left the meeting and shook hands with each of the men, one gray-haired gentleman put a note in my hand. As we got back in the car, I looked at the note. It was a five-dollar bill. They were having a gasoline war, so gas was sixteen cents per gallon, rather than the normal twenty-five cents per gallon. God took us home, and although we were rejected, God knew we needed that special assurance, and the *hand of the Lord* was taking care of us.

We accepted the board's counsel and moved to Perth, New York, where we lived with my parents in a small house at Youth Bible Congress. They were working at the camp as bookkeeper and secretary. We began going door-to-door in Amsterdam, New York, taking a religious survey, hoping this would provide us opportunities for personal evangelism and experience in witnessing. During this time, a retired Methodist pastor was keeping two small churches open in communities along the Sacandaga Reservoir. One was in North Hampton and the other in Edinburg, about fifteen minutes apart. After the pastor was hospitalized with a heart attack, his wife asked if I would preach at both churches. God opened this door for us to gain experience in preparation for the mission field. It was winter, and the road was often covered with snow and ice, making it difficult to travel. I would preach at North Hampton first. As you went in the front door, there were two iron wood stoves in the back of the church. These wood stoves would be fired up, but not nearly enough to warm up the church. People sat with their overcoats on. A black sheet metal flue ran from the stove in the back to the chimney in the front of the church, acting like a hot radiator as the heat went through the pipe and out the chimney. Our fellowship was limited to before the service, because as soon as we said the benediction, we had to leave to get to the Edinburg church and start the second service. Each congregation consisted of twenty-five to thirty people. They shared their offerings with us, which helped us with our living expenses. We enjoyed our time sharing God's Word with these people. The Lord was so good in providing these opportunities to serve and gain experience.

After about a year, we once again applied to Christian Missions, and in May 1950, we were appointed to the Niger Colony of French West Africa. That summer, we again worked at Youth Bible Congress in Perth as counselors. We met wonderful people there, which in turn gave us contacts with local churches. Some of these churches financially supported us monthly. Three of them have continued until this writing, over sixty years! Again we see the wisdom of the godly board who delayed our appointment, and how the Lord used these months of experience to form friendships and bonding with people and churches.

Our next hurdle was getting our required monthly support and our outfit and passage money. It seemed like a lot of money at the time, but again we knew God would provide. While working that summer at YBC, we received a letter from Mr. Eugene Wiedoff, a member of the Bridgeport Baptist Church where Elaine and I were members. He said God had put upon his heart to support us with $150 per month. The mission was requiring us to have $55 a month for each of us and $20 per month for David Jr.—a total of $130.00. We would be oversupported by $20. Mr. Wiedoff had been a welder at the navy shipyard in Philadelphia during the war. He was known as "Whiskers," as he refused to shave until the end of World War II. He was a bit eccentric but had started a nursing home for the aged. He began his support immediately and also provided us with tools and other equipment that we would need in Africa. So instead of needing to raise monthly support during deputation that fall, our emphasis was prayer support and our outfit and passage. We confined our deputation to the upper New York area. In 1950, you could call a pastor and request a meeting for any day of the week and almost always it could be scheduled. If it were a Monday, Tuesday, Thursday, or Friday, it usually was combined with a carry-in dinner. Services started at 8:00 PM and ended between 9:00 and 9:30. No one was in a hurry to leave. A freewill offering was taken, and this always covered travel expenses and left a balance for outfit and passage. By November 1950, we had our outfit purchased and crated.

Shipping containers didn't exist in those days, so our crates were wooden, which would later become our cupboards in Africa. Our furniture needed to be metal, or otherwise it would be eaten by termites. Dishes and clothing were packed in fifty-five-gallon drums that later would serve as water barrels in the kitchen and bathroom, since there would be no running water. Elaine packed drinking glasses in Wonder Bread bags to cushion them. When we unpacked them in Timbuktu, the glasses all had the familiar red, yellow, and blue circles nicely imprinted on them from the Wonder Bread bags. Food also would be stored in steel drums to keep out the mice, rats, lizards, ants, and termites.

Before leaving for Africa, we made a trip to the Chicago area. The Wednesday evening before Thanksgiving, we had a meeting at the First Baptist Church in Rochester, Michigan. The newscasters were predicting a snowstorm for Thanksgiving Day, so after our meeting, we decided to travel all night to be with Elaine's brother, Wilbur, and her sister-in-law, Lorraine. Wilbur was starting a church south of Chicago. The church was meeting in a fire station and had scheduled a Thanksgiving morning service. After the service, we received the Western Union telegram that we had been anxiously anticipating. We were scheduled to sail on a freighter on December 2. We did not linger for turkey with the Beswicks, as we had a long trip back to Elaine's parents' house in Bridgeport, Pennsylvania, and much to do with less than a week before we would sail.

That storm that had been predicted did indeed blow in as we traveled on old U.S. Highway 30 across Indiana and Ohio. Ohio, Indiana, southern Michigan, and western Pennsylvania were declared to be in a "state of emergency." I got to a stretch of road that had not been plowed, so I turned around and took Elaine and David Jr. (now nicknamed Butch) into the nearest town, and I put them on a train to Paoli, Pennsylvania. Paoli was close to Bridgeport and was where the steam engines would be fitted with an electric engine before going into Philadelphia. After seeing them off and phoning her father to meet them in Paoli, I tried again to drive the old Plymouth sedan that had been loaned to us but got stuck in the snow. A kind farmer towed me into his barnyard, along with several other stranded people, and kept us in his house overnight. The next afternoon, a snowplow broke through and opened one lane of traffic. I finally made it to the Pennsylvania turnpike. The eastern terminus was at Valley Forge. When I exited at Valley Forge and paid my toll, I was told that I was the first to come all the way across the turnpike. When I exited the turnpike on route 202, my front wheel was smoking and squealing. I had burned out a wheel bearing, only a few miles from my in-laws. I drove slowly to their house, where I was met by Elaine and Butch. My father-in-law, a good mechanic, found new wheel bearings and repaired the car.

The week passed quickly. It was cold and drizzling when we arrived at the Brooklyn docks in New York City that Saturday morning for our 9:00

AM departure. About forty people met us, with their umbrellas opening and closing with the sporadic showers. Besides our parents and siblings, people had come from our home church in Bridgeport and others from Perth and YBC. Margaret McCaba pinned a beautiful corsage on Elaine's overcoat and presented us with a box of Whitman's chocolates.

We were allowed to have three hundred pounds of baggage per person to take aboard the ship. We were headed for Algeria, a territory of France at the time, where we would study French and learn about the Islamic religion. We took enough to set up basic housekeeping in Algeria, but our freight would be shipped later to Niger.

Wilber and Edna Barnes and their six-month-old baby son Steve sailed with us. They were older than us, perhaps by ten years. They also were headed to Algeria but would remain in Algeria as missionaries.

When 9:00 AM rolled around, cargo was still being loaded on the ship. The French ship, called the *Foria,* was an old cargo ship that had been used during WWII. The crew was French, but the stewards and cooks were Chinese. There were twelve passengers, the maximum permitted without a medical doctor on board. We were permitted to go on board about 9:30. Our cabins were in the front of the ship on the starboard side, high above the main deck and just under the bridge. There were two bunks with an armoire and enough room for a folding crib for Butch. Butch was now a year and a half old. Next to our cabin was a small lounge with a phonograph machine, and next to it in the center of the ship was the dining room for the captain, other officers, and twelve passengers.

At ten o'clock, Joe McCaba conducted a farewell service. We crowded into the dining room, spilling into the lounge. He committed us to the Lord for our trip and future ministry. Our friends disembarked down the long, narrow gangway, and we hugged and kissed good-bye through the tears, knowing it would be five years before we could see them again. My mother particularly would get emotional at times. As for me, I didn't have a hard time leaving. I was rather independent. I had joined the navy at seventeen years old, I worked at camp away from family, and I had visited Africa while in the navy, and so I was more excited than sad. The hardest thing was seeing the reaction of my mother, with her red face and tears. The support of people from our home church was so encouraging that it made leaving easier too. We knew God was sending us, and we were excited to be a part of His plan.

The whole group waited on the pier below, waiting for the last cargo to be loaded. They wanted to watch the tugboats pull us out and wave good-bye as we sailed out of sight. This did not happen, as more and more trucks pulled out onto the dock to be unloaded. We finally went ashore again to be with our friends, and at 3:00 PM, we encouraged them to go home. A few friends stayed, and we waved good-bye to them when we finally sailed at 10:00 PM.

Chapter 3.

Off to Africa

And when they had fasted and prayed, and laid their hands on them, they sent them away. Acts 13:3

When we woke on Sunday morning, we needed our sea legs, as the ship began to rock, roll, and heave just enough to cause some nausea. But we got a reprieve from the cold winter weather when we entered the balmy Gulf Stream. This lasted for a day or so before we were back sailing on the frigid North Atlantic.

We shared a dining room table with the Barneses. The other six passengers sat together. Five were French, and the sixth was a young Spaniard. The captain, observing that we prayed and thanked the Lord for our food before each meal, told us in broken English that he was an atheist and that there was no God.

When we prayed, we had no idea what we were thanking the Lord for. We knew it was food, but the French ate things that we had never eaten before. It seemed like they started at one end of a cow and went to the other end. We had a small French/English dictionary, so each day we would pick up the menu and try to figure out what we were going to be served that day. It didn't take us long to figure out that the French had fancy names for their dishes that did not tell you much. For example, *"bouche a la rein"* means "mouth of the queen." In reality, it was cooked brains in a flaky pastry shell with white sauce. The next meal was tongue, then tripe, then blood sausage, kidneys, and ox tail. Wow! As twenty-two-year-old kids, we did not recognize this as culture shock, but we were certainly shocked. When trying to figure out how to eat an artichoke, we just watched the captain eat his and soon learned that you don't eat the leaves but rather scrape the end of them between your teeth to extract the small soft part of the leaf after you have soaked it in vinegar and oil. It's a lot of work, but fun! Then you finally get to the thistle that only a camel would enjoy, but hidden under that was the heart that was delicious with more vinegar and oil. They should have given us a discount, as we did not touch their wine. (The mission's principles and practices forbid the missionaries from drinking alcohol.)

On the fifth day at sea, we encountered a terrible North Atlantic storm. In the dining room, all of the chairs were fastened down with turnbuckles. The tables had been attached to the deck. Racks were placed on the tables and secured. These racks held the dishes and glasses from crashing to the deck. Only about half of the passengers showed up for meals. Along with the sound of the wind and the waves hitting the sides of the ship, it was not uncommon to hear passengers heaving with nothing more to bring up. Because our cabin was high up, just under the bridge, the hatches were not water tight, because it was assumed waves would not reach that height. The marine architects were wrong, and with thirty-foot waves, we ended up with about four inches of water slopping back and forth in our cabin.

We put our foot locker and suitcases on the bunk. Elaine and I were sick as dogs, but Butch was enjoying being thrown from one bulkhead to the other. For him it was like being in bumper cars at an amusement park. He did end up with his first black eye. Then the real problem began in the ship's hull. Down in the middle hold, bundles of sheet metal broke loose and began sliding back and forth across the decking, crashing into the sides of the ship. To make things worse, there was a large transformer destined for Alexandria, Egypt. The steel hit the transformer and broke it, causing oil to spill out, making the deck more slippery than ice. Crew members frantically and fearfully tried to lash down the steel. The transformer was so tall that some of the decking had to be left off to accommodate it in the hold, thus we could see the men below struggling to secure the steel and at the same time save their own lives. Our atheist captain came to us, explaining that his weather instruments did not agree with the weather conditions, and he asked us to pray! He did not need to ask. Seeing his men risking their lives trying to save the ship and seeing the fear on the captain's face, we had already begun praying. We experienced another day of rough seas before arriving in Porto, Portugal.

In the ship's lounge, there was a record player, but the only record I remember hearing was a Spanish song called "Manana" that the young Spaniard played over and over again. He was supposed to disembark in

Lisbon, but the moment the ship touched land in Porto, he disappeared. We all had sea sickness, but his had been the worst. We understood his desire to "jump" ship, get onto *terra firma,* and head for home. In Porto, bundles of cork were loaded on the main deck high enough to obstruct our view. Our next port of call was Lisbon. As we pulled into port, we passed an enormous sailing vessel with its sails full as the light breeze filled them. It looked like an artist's painting. I was surprised that vessels like this still sailed the seas.

We went ashore, trying to learn how to walk again on solid ground. I walked through the streets looking for some snacks to take back aboard. Our box of chocolates was long gone. I remember discovering long, thin nuts in a cellophane bag—pine nuts. Our next stop was Casablanca. I had been in this exotic city four years earlier while in the navy. Its boulevards were lined with Royal Palms and flanked with expensive shops and sidewalk cafes. The men wore the traditional long gowns, turbans, bloomer-like trousers, and pointed shoes that looked like a cross between a shoe and a sandal. The back was folded down inside so they could be slipped on or you could walk out of them. They were convenient for slipping off when going into the mosques but so similar in looks that I wondered how they knew whose were whose after they finished their prayers. Edna Barnes was not familiar with Arab dress. She needed a bathroom and assumed that these long, white-gowned people were women. She followed one of them into the facility, where she was immediately chased out. She told the story after we all got back on our ship. We laughed. Again it was culture shock, but we did not recognize it as such. We just saw it as funny!

Some new cars were unloaded in Casablanca. We held our breath as we watched the longshoremen unloading the vehicles. It seemed like some of the longshoremen had family members who owned body shops, as several of the cars hit the side of the ship while unloading, causing body damage.

Our next stop was Tangiers. Before arriving at the "free" port, our portable Corona typewriter broke. We hoped that during our brief stay we would find a repair shop. We arrived just before noon. Elaine and Butch stayed on board, and I, with the typewriter in hand, began trekking through the streets and alleyways, looking for a typewriter store. The free port charged no taxes or duties, so it was bustling. I finally found a typewriter shop, but to my dismay, it was closed. In fact, everything was closed, and again the culture shock kicked in. It was siesta time, and nothing would move again until after two o'clock. I waited patiently, but then I began hearing the ship blowing its big, boisterous horn. I decided I better get back to the ship a mile or so away. In the meantime, Elaine told the captain that I was in town. With his French accent, he simply told Elaine, "Madame, this is a cargo ship, not a passenger ship. We wait for cargo, but we do not wait for passengers." She was in tears and frantic as she watched the men take the lines off of the huge bits on the deck. Finally, as the last line was being taken off, I arrived dockside with unfixed typewriter and jumped onto the ship and into Elaine's arms, with tears running down her cheeks.

Algiers: Meeting Missionaries

We arrived in Algiers in the evening. Earlier we'd had the unique experience of seeing two continents as we passed through the Straits of Gibraltar—Africa on the right and Europe on the left. The docks were full, so we anchored just off shore until a berth came available. After dark, while looking toward the city, we noticed a small boat coming toward the ship. To our surprise and delight, as it approached the side of the ship, we heard, "Hello, Hello." It was the voices of our missionaries, John Aseltine and Dallas Washer. Edna Barnes called down to them, "We know some French," and she proudly said, "Mercy," which brought a laugh from them. She was trying to say *merci*, the French word for thank you, but her accent was definitely American. They came aboard the ship. We had a good time getting to know them. John asked us if we had anything to declare. We assured them that we only had personal effects except, that on the dock in New York, Ida King from the Bridgeport Church had handed me a Turkish towel, and wrapped within it was a .38-caliber revolver. Eugene Wiedoff had given it to her to bring to our sailing, as he was unable to come to New York. John immediately exclaimed, "You can't take that ashore without a permit."

I said, "It's not a problem. I'll just throw it overboard."

"No! Don't do that. If you don't want it, I'll take it. We'll give it to the customs officer to hold while I apply for a permit."

The next morning, a tugboat approached and slipped us into our berth. John arrived at ten o'clock. He had arranged for a taxi to take our baggage. We completed paperwork with the immigration service and customs people, having surrendered the gun. We had just completed twenty-two days aboard the *Foria*, and in two days, we would celebrate Christmas in Algeria. I don't know how we did it, but John got us all into his car—three Barneses and three Marshalls. The car was an old Berliet, the only Berliet

I ever saw. It was probably manufactured in the 1930s. Berliets were still making huge trucks, but they certainly did not manufacture cars during or after WW II.

The trip took us through Algiers, a beautiful city of contrasts. Most buildings were Moorish in design, but the downtown business section resembled the Champs Elysee in Paris. Algeria was home to millions of *Pied Noires*, or French people who were born and raised in Algeria, a French protectorate. The official language was French, but Arabic was the dominant language among the people. Most women were veiled and dressed in very modest clothing. Men generally wore a red fez on their head, whether or not they were dressed in their traditional style or had adopted European dress.

We passed through the suburbs where "souks"—small shops specialized in their merchandise—lined the main streets. Passing by the meat stores, we saw those who sold beef, others horse meat (for the French), and others lamb. The lamb shops had the heads of sheep and goats hanging from a metal hook or threaded by a rope.

Then there were the charcuterie, which specialized in pork. These shops had fancy sausages and hams, and of course catered to the French or non-Muslims. Patisseries sold bread, croissants, and other goodies. The long baguettes were handled by many hands, as customers would feel the French bread to see if it crackled when squeezed. It had to have just the right feel and sound. After buying, it customers slipped the baguette under their armpit and carried it home, sometimes nibbling on it en route.

On our way to the Arab village of Souma, we passed through the city of Bufarik, where we would do most of our shopping. The road was straight, with a slight incline, and would terminate at the base of the Atlas Mountains. Just before the end of the road, about a half mile outside of Souma, was a farm with olive trees and several variations of fruit and citrus trees. This is where we would live. The farm was owned by Mr. and Mrs. Seltzer. They were about the age of our parents. Mrs. Seltzer grew up in South Africa where her parents had been missionaries, so she spoke English, which was a great blessing. We lived in an apartment over a wagon shed on the end of an olive mill. On the other end of the mill was a small house where the Aseltines lived with their three children and where the Barneses would live with their seven-month-old son, Steven. The olive mill was built on the side of a hill so that our apartment on the second floor opened up at ground level as you went out the back kitchen door.

On Christmas day, we all got together for a Christmas dinner prepared by Doris Aseltine, John's wife. We were joined by Dan and Ann Zimmerman. The Zimmermans had completed their language study and were waiting for their visas to serve in Niger. A young Arab lad known as Jackson also joined us. As a boy, he mingled with the American soldiers based in Algeria during World War II and learned English from them. He also learned to play Ping-Pong, so Christmas afternoon we played Ping-Pong in the small yard at the Aseltines.

On New Year's Eve, we all went to the Algiers airport known as Maison Blanc to bid farewell to the Washers as they boarded a small airplane bound for Niger. Everybody at the airport was celebrating the New Year. The crew of the plane sat at the bar drinking out the old and celebrating the New Year. Shortly after midnight, as the champagne was being gulped, the call came for everyone to board the plane. The Washers were the only ones who did not stagger aboard. We waited for their plane to take off. They would fly out over the Mediterranean Sea, where they would have to circle several times to gain sufficient altitude to clear the Atlas Mountains before heading south across the Sahara Desert. We prayed before they left and committed them to the Lord for a safe flight. Certainly only the Lord could do this, as the pilots were not in any shape to get them there safely. We arrived back home at 2:00 AM.

Our language teacher, Madame Tavel, was Mrs. Seltzer's sister. She lived about four miles away on the road from Souma to the city of Blida. We purchased a Velo Solex motorbike for transportation to and from our lessons. This was a popular French bicycle that had a small, two-cycle engine hinged over the front wheel. You started out by pedaling the bike and then lowering the motor, which had a wheel on it to meet the tire, thus providing friction and turning the front wheel. (The French were the forerunners of the "front wheel drive.") I soon discovered that the little engine was designed for one person, so was not practical for a family. I would go to Bufarik to buy mutton and beef at a French butcher shop (complete with sheep heads in the window for people to buy to cook up to make sauces). When I would return home, the road looked level but actually had a slight incline. I would be pedaling as fast as I could but be passed by Arabs on bicycles with no motors. I was peddling and using the motor at the same time and could not keep up with them. It was so discouraging and embarrassing! I dreaded that ride into town to shop. Along the road was a large property fenced in by airplane propellers collected from spare part depots for U.S. planes during WWII.

Within a couple of weeks, I received a letter from Dal Washer asking me to purchase a Velo Solex and ship it to Niger. I offered to sell him mine at a good price, and he agreed, so I shipped it to him. In Niger, there were no paved roads, and thus it would serve him well as he traveled slowly over the washboard dirt and gravel roads. I replaced it with a small Peugot with a sturdy rack for baggage. The store where I purchased the cycle also sold a seat made to attach to the rack, along with a pedal-like foot rest. Now we had a family vehicle. Butch would sit on the gas tank, I was in the driver's seat, and Elaine was on the seat behind me. This would be our vehicle for the next three years until the family outgrew it.

After a little over a month, Dan and Ann Zimmerman left Algeria for Niger and eventually moved to Gao in the French Soudan. Then Roger Bacon, a single man also headed for Niger, arrived for language study. John Aseltine had arranged for Roger to live with a French family in Boufaric about five kilometers[1] down the same road that we lived on.

In March, we went to Algiers to welcome Muriel Vanderlip and Madeliene Campbell. These ladies were both from Ontario, Canada, and had graduated from the London Bible College. They arrived on a passenger ship, and it was obvious that the Atlantic was not very kind to them. Madeliene looked like she had not eaten for over a week, and I think she had already determined that this was the last time she would travel by ship. She would find other ways to feed the fish.

Mildred Dibble had just completed her first term in Niger and had decided to take her first month of furlough with a friend in Algiers before going back to the States. She came out to spend a couple days with us. We were playing a game of Monopoly one evening when a knock came at the door. It was John Aseltine, who said, "Come quickly, there is a thief in the olive mill."

There was a door from our apartment into the mill, but we went down the outside stairway and to the back of the mill. We noticed that the thief had removed several tiles to enter the mill. The roof sloped into the hill behind the mill so that the roof on the backside was only three feet from the ground. En route to the back of the mill, we noticed that the electricity had gone off. We assumed that the thief had cut the belt to the generator. This was attached to a mechanism powered by a water turbine from an irrigation ditch farther up the hill. The irrigation water was diverted at

---

1   We use kilometers throughout the book, since that is the unit we used throughout our travels (1 kilometer = 0.62 miles; 1 mile = 1.6 kilometers).

night to run through the mill to provide electricity to give light to the apartments and the Seltzers' home.

John retrieved a baseball bat, which he placed in my hands. He had the 38 pistol. As we approached the hole in the roof in total darkness, he yelled for the thief to come out. There was dead silence, so John fired a couple rounds into the hole. Then he said, "I'm going to get Mr. Seltzer. You club the thief with the bat if he comes out of the hole."

John shot a couple more rounds in the air while going up the road to rouse Mr. Seltzer. They soon arrived with flashlights. Mr. Seltzer entered the mill and discovered the thief had left with about five gallons of olive oil. Thank the Lord the thief had escaped before we got to the hole in the roof, because if I had wacked somebody in the head with the bat, I might be writing my memoirs from an Algerian prison. Or if I had been convicted of murder, I may have been executed by the guillotine, which was still used for executions at this time in France and its colonies. I don't know if John ever had another occasion to fire the pistol that had been given to me by Eugene Wiedoff through Ida King that rainy day in Brooklyn, New York. What I do know was that the *hand of the Lord* was upon us! And the thief was caught the next day in Souma, and several large cans of olive oil were retrieved.

Language study was going very slowly for me, and one day as Madame Tavel was trying to get me to correctly pronounce the word "attention" and I continued to pronounce it as in English. She turned to me and said, "Mr. Marshall, I think you should have learned English before trying French." She was right! Language learning was not my gift!

Algiers was not the best place to study French, especially in a rural area where Arabic was the spoken language. But Joe McCaba insisted that our missionaries do their language study in Algeria, first of all because he did not want us rubbing shoulders with missionaries from other mission organizations. He feared that we might "jump ship." This was valid, especially when we had so many single missionaries who might find a mate with another mission. Second, he wanted us to be exposed to the culture and religion of Islam. A third reason was that he had a French friend who was a pastor in the Reformed church who also had some political ties with the government who could be influential in helping with visas and other government paperwork.

I got to the point where I felt I needed a more structured French language school. Most missionaries from other organizations either went to Paris or to Switzerland for their language training. I mentioned to John

Aseltine my desire to go to France to a language school. His first response was, "Joe will never agree to that."

Then I said, "I still have some G.I. Bill schooling that I can take, and the language school in Paris is on the approved list. Do you think if I propose giving my $55 per month support to the home office and I live on my government subsidy that Joe would let us go?"

John's immediate response was, "He'll let you go!"

I wrote the home office and got an immediate response giving us permission to go. We had friends, Tom and Fern Wilson, who were in language school in Paris. They were missionaries with the North Africa Mission and had been classmates of ours in Bible school. In fact, it was Tom's sister, Betty, who had invited me to join the Africa prayer group at school. We immediately began corresponding with them, requesting help in getting information about language school and housing. We soon heard back, and they found a place for us to live in the same boarding house where they were living only three blocks from the Alliance Francaise, the language school. With this answer to prayer, we could see the *hand of the Lord* in providing for us, as housing was extremely difficult to find in Paris.

Our next challenge was to get to France. A passenger ship with four classes went between Algiers and Marseille. Because the trip only took about twenty-three hours, we decided on fourth class, which was all we could afford anyway. It was nine dollars per person, and Butch was free. We were told the accommodations were in the vessel's hold, but we would have access to the main deck, where we could rent deck chairs. We arrived at the dock in Algiers about 1:00 PM. As we waited on the dock, they called for the first-class passengers, and we watched them go up the gangway and find their cabins, then the second class, and then the third class. The third class was a dormitory-type room with bunks. But then we were shocked to see the passenger gangway removed, a larger hatch opened, and another gangway put in place. As we watched in amazement, about fifty horses were led into the ship, along with bales of hay. Then the PA system on the ship blared out, inviting the fourth-class passengers aboard. We went up the same gangway and through the same hatch as the horses, taking care not to step on the fresh manure as we boarded. It was a mad rush, with a couple hundred Arabs running with their long, flowing gowns, each trying to mark out twice as much room on the deck as they needed. We sat on our footlockers separated by a bulkhead from the horses. We had brought a picnic lunch with us, but with no ventilation, the atmosphere was not conducive for a picnic. Within an hour, we hit into stormy weather, so we couldn't go top side for fresh air because the waves were crashing over the bow of the ship.

It was Ramandan, so the Muslims were fasting during the daylight hours. They are not allowed to even swallow their own saliva, and thus they were constantly spitting as they clear their throats. This added to the problem of walking on the steel decking, as it became a large, slippery spittoon. Moreover, because of the rough weather, many fourth-class passengers became seasick, adding to the already slimy deck.

More than once we thought about the folks in third, second, and first class in their comfortable staterooms or even the dormitory. We wondered what the dining rooms looked like and whether the air-conditioned lounges were nice. On the other hand, we were having the time of our lives. What an experience to be surrounded by Arabs, clearing their throats and vomiting the night's previous lavish meal. We felt like Jonah in the belly of the great fish. Finally, at sunset, to make matters worse, it was prayer time. Prior to praying, everyone filled their kettles with water and then proceeded to wash their feet and hands, etc. Add that to the metal deck and you end up with a lot of slush. Our watches were checked at least fifty times during this twenty-three-hour test of survival. There was a rest room, but you dared not use it for fear of dying while holding your breath. Finally, after twenty-three hours of no sleep, we arrived in Marseille. What a relief!

In Marseille, we boarded the train for Paris. We were in third class, but it seemed like first class after what we had just experienced. We slept most of the nine- or ten-hour trip.

Preparing in Paris

Tom and Fern met us at the train station. We took a taxi to the *Pension Lagnamous*. The pension, or boarding house, was located on the third floor of a large building located directly across the street from the Jardin du Luxemburg, a beautiful park with shade, benches, and swings.

We climbed the steps, entered the door of the third floor, and went down the hall to our room. Our room had a double bed and a cot that Butch used. The communal toilet was located at the end of the hall. The bathtub was also communal and located at the opposite end of the hall. However, the bath could only be used on Saturday or Sunday, as the maids used the bathtub during the week to wash sheets and towels. If you wanted a bath on the weekend, you had to sign up on a sheet of paper for a particular time.

Our bed had a straw mattress and a long, straw-filled roll for a pillow. The sheets felt like burlap, and the bottom sheet was washed in the bath tub at the end of the hall every two weeks. The top sheet became the bottom sheet when the bottom sheet went to the tub. Our room had a small sink. If you wanted warm water, you had to get up early before the other twenty-four boarders. Water was heated from midnight until 5:00 AM in a twenty-gallon tank because the electric rates were inexpensive during the night hours. Needless to say, it did not take long for people to use twenty gallons of water. Breakfast was served each morning on a metal platter and left on the floor at your door. It consisted of either tea or coffee with hot milk, along with a couple pieces of French bread and with some butter, which had been scraped to look like a snail.

There was no lunch, but at suppertime, we all sat at a long table for dinner at 8:00 PM. Soup was always the first course, along with bread. Butter was only served at breakfast. The gentleman who sat directly across from me had a full-grown French poodle that sat next to his master and shared his dinner, including his soup. They shared the only soup spoon taking turns—a spoonful of soup for the master and a spoonful of soup for his dog. Fridays always featured fish soup, with the head of the fish in your bowl looking eye to eye with you. Soup was generally run through a *passoir* (sieve), so you did not know the contents, but it was very tasty. The main course could be horse steak, blood sausage, or beef stew. In fact, the reason for the Algerian horses going to France with us on our ship was that the French eat a lot of horse meat, especially ground. The meal ended with cheese and fruit or pudding. Once the complete meal was served, the maids disappeared until the next morning. The dishes and silverware remained on the table, and two or three cats immediately jumped on the table to wash the dishes and clean up any food that had not been consumed. The next morning, the maids gathered up the dishes and held them under the faucet, allowing the water to cascade over them. Of course, the hot water was already used up about two hours earlier. Fortunately, we were provided with a cloth napkin, so it was traditional to see everyone wipe off their plate and polish the silverware before eating. The meals were served family style. We never thought of this experience as a cultural shock but just amusing.

We were in the habit of having lunch at noon, so we made a snack of French bread with butter and jam, along with honey. Peanut butter could be found in a health store. It was made in Dakar, Senegal, West Africa. Its consistency was very different and light in color, and it appeared to have some shells in it. Our budget was limited, so we had to be very careful that we did not splurge. That was very difficult, as the bread store also sold French pastry. *Wow,* how tantalizing! We did manage a couple times a week to buy a "pomier," a flat, flaky pastry in the shape of an apple that was drenched in honey. There were no bread wrappers, and bread was carried under the armpits. I don't know if it became better tasting, but it was good. Instead of bottles, everyone had an aluminum milk container, either one or two liters, which you took to the milk store. The proprietor dipped the milk with a ladle from a large can and filled your container. It was neither pasteurized nor homogenized. The milk store also sold cheese. We came to enjoy French cheeses, especially Camembert on French bread—the runnier the better. Gruyere in cooking was a favorite.

After a few months at our boarding house, we found another one with a much larger room on the ground floor for the same price. It was the only place that would allow a child. Most housing or boarding houses would not allow children. Dogs and cats were allowed, but not children. Another advantage was that the owner lived in the rooms directly above our room, which meant that the radiator for our room was supplied by the same hot water as his rooms. Generally in France, the heat in winter was not determined by the outside temperature but by the date. Rooms and apartments got heat from November 15 until March 15, no exceptions. Our heat came from coal furnaces in the cellar. The coal was delivered in a large wagon drawn by beautiful Belgian Clydesdale horses. I had never seen such big animals. The other big advantage that we had in living at the Residence Jeanne was that we had hot water all day and a shower and toilet room on the second floor. Often in France, the toilets are in a separate room from the bathroom. The second floor was actually what we would consider the third floor. In Europe, the first floor is called the ground floor, and what we would call the second floor is considered the first floor. A small, caged elevator would accommodate two people as they moved between five floors and the attic for the housekeepers.

The dining area was on the ground floor just beyond our room. It was here that I saw a baby in a small bassinet drinking from a baby bottle that had no milk in it but diluted wine. Apparently there are no age limits in France as to when you can consume alcoholic beverages. The Residence Jeanne did not serve meals on Sunday, but we had a door in our room that went directly to a kitchenette equipped with a small two-burner gas hotplate.

When we were married in 1948, we were given a Revereware four-quart pressure cooker by my parents, and it has followed us for the past sixty years, and thus our Sunday meals were cooked right next to our room. We had individual small family tables, and the menu was the same each week, so you knew what day you would be served horsemeat. Within a couple months, Madeliene Campbell and Muriel Vanderlip decided to leave Algeria. We procured a room for them at the Residence Jeanne. On Sundays, we all ate together in our room. On Sunday mornings. we attended Avenue du Maine Baptist Church, which was within walking distance. On Sunday afternoons, an English service was held in a large chateau occupied by an American naval officer. He had access to American food, and after the services, he and his wife always had a big spread of food. Typically thirty-five to fifty missionaries and other American Christians living in the Paris area attended. The naval officer was later transferred to Naples, Italy, but in the Lord's providence, the Greater European Mission began a work in the same area with Bob and Jeanette Evans. They started the European Bible school. I had met Bob years before when he was based in Norfolk, Virginia, and my ship anchored off shore there on weekends. I had attended several Navigators meetings at which Bob was involved.

We enjoyed our stay in Paris and learned to navigate the underground Metro system. As with other means of transportation, it had its class system but only two classes, first and second. First class was the car in the middle, and second was the first two and last two cars. Elaine was pregnant, but there were reserved seats for pregnant women and wounded veterans. Most people would stand holding on to the overhead straps. This exposed a lot of armpits to the air with very little deodorant. The French are known for their perfumes, but these were the early years after World War II, and perfume was a low priority, as people had little spending money. We enjoyed listening to the musicians who played musical instruments for tips in the Metro. Accordions, violins, and saxophones were popular. Not only would you find these people in the subways but often in the streets that were lined with boarding houses, where they hoped for showers of coins from the open windows above.

We had fun taking the metro to large department stores, such as Au Printemp and Le Bon Samaritan. Butch enjoyed going to the top floor, where they had salons to coiffeur the dogs. It was quite a show looking through the glass barrier watching them bathe the French poodles and then trim, cut, and brush them. They left the salon with pompoms on their tails and around their ankles, polished nails, and trimmed bangs.

Paris is the city of lights, and we enjoyed visiting Paris at night, seeing and photographing the many historical buildings and monuments, which were lit up so that we could take slides at night. Colored film such as ASA10 Kodachrome was very slow, so it was not unusual for me to set up a tripod in the middle of the Champs d' Elysses for several seconds while taking time exposures of the Arc de Triumph or the Obelisk in the middle of the Place de Concorde. There were few vehicles other than the prewar taxis. Most people traveled on bicycles, Vespa scooters, Velo Solex motorized bikes, or buses.

We enjoyed going up the Eiffel Tower with Butch and taking his picture with the city as a background, as so many millions have done before and after us. We were humiliated when in the large room in the Arc de Triumph Butch needed to use a restroom. None could be found, and he could no longer contain himself. We were immediately accosted by a uniformed guard shouting at the top of his voice with every tourist in the room listening as he said, *"Votre fils a fait pepe sur la gloire de la France!"* (Your son pee-peed on the glory of France!") We had to act like we were dumb tourists and did not understand what he said. Needless to say, we looked for the elevator and escaped, with our two-and-a-half-year-old, and got lost in the crowds walking the Champ d'Elysses.

We celebrated out second Christmas away from home with a small Christmas tree in our bedroom. Santa Claus in France was not our familiar, round, pot-bellied, jolly St. Nick. His clothes were similar, but he had a thirty-two-inch waist instead of a fifty-two. Maybe the food shortage during the war took its toll on Santa.

By January 1952, my brother Frank and his wife Eleanor applied to Christians Mission and were leaving for their language study. We got a room for them in the same boarding house with us. But we began to look for another place where we could share a furnished house together. We found a very nice house on the outskirts of Paris. The house had a quaint name, Villa Pazilla. It was owned by an Italian gentlemen who often went to the States on business, and on one occasion, he even visited my parents in Perth, New York.

When we arrived in France, our living allowance was sent to us via the French American Banking Corporation in New York City and was transferred to us through a bank in Paris. The French had put an exchange rate of one dollar per 350 French Francs. On the "black market," you could get five hundred French francs per dollar. It was illegal to change money on the "black market," so in effect, the French banks were profiting 150 francs on every dollar you changed, plus the commission they charged in making the exchange. We learned that if you went across the border into Switzerland, you could get 500 to 510 francs for a U. S. dollar. We also learned it was illegal to take French francs out of France without a permit, but there was no law against taking dollars out, and there was no law against bringing French francs into France. It didn't take long to realize that we were losing about 40 percent of our money by exchanging in France. At this time, all of Christian Missions missionaries were serving in French colonies of Algeria, Martinique, Niger, and French Sudan, plus those of us who were in France for language study.

Tom Clark was the mission treasurer, and after explaining this to him, he would send me a monthly check for all the missionaries with a list of the amounts for each field. When the check arrived, I would take a train to Bale, Switzerland, and go to the bank, where they would accept the check. They had a dressing stall in the basement where I would stash the enormous amount of cash into a money belt that Elaine had made for me, head for the train station, and go back to Paris. There I would jump onto my motorcycle and head for home. The next day I would go to the Post Office and make out money orders and send them to each field. The French had an excellent postal system, and within a couple of days, each field had their money with about a 40 percent bonus, all of it perfectly legal, but a bit risky for me traveling with all of that cash.

Spring 1952 was a special time for us. Songs like "I Love Paris in the Springtime" and "April in Paris" attempt to capture the magic of the season there. The gardens and parks in Paris bloom and are manicured. Trees are trimmed and stand tall at attention like soldiers awaiting the bulbs to spring forth as a color guard on a tapestry of design. In the middle of April, Eleanor, my sister-in-law, gave birth to their firstborn son, Robert, to be followed by Elaine giving birth to our first daughter, Sandra the day after Butch celebrated his third birthday on May 1. Sandy was born at the American Hospital in Paris. Elaine's doctor was in Algeria attending a medical conference, but that didn't matter, as doctors in France had very little experience in delivering babies. This was the expertise of a *"sage femme"* midwife. Sandy seemed half grown, as she was nearly a ten-pound girl. Breastfeeding was normal and very public in France. To check on the amount of milk the baby was getting, you rented a baby scale at the local pharmacy. Before each feeding, the baby was laid in the canvas sling on the scale, and you slid the weight on the bar until it balanced and you would then write the number of kilos and grams. At the end of feeding, the same procedure was followed, and then you calculated the difference.

The Villa Pazilla had a lovely garden, and being on the side of a steep hill, it was terraced. On each level, a reservoir of water existed where gardeners filled buckets to water the flowers. While I was at the hospital visiting Elaine and Sandy, Butch leaned over too far and fell into one of these reservoirs and nearly drowned. The *hand of the Lord* was there in the form of a little French playmate who had presence of mind to pull him up and get his head out of the water.

Two weeks after Sandy's birth, we applied for our visas to proceed to AOF (Afrique Occidental Francaise) French West Africa. This required getting shots at the Institute Louis Pasteur for yellow fever, measles, and a vaccination for smallpox for baby Sandy and a physical for Elaine and I and Butch. Shots in France were never given in the arm but in the buttocks. Needles generally were sterilized by pouring a little alcohol over them and then torched with a match. Needless to say, Sandy's target area was small, so the vaccination for smallpox was given on the sole of Sandy's little foot. This would leave a rather large scar. (I guess they didn't want the scar to show when she competed for Miss America.)

The physical was something else! One doctor apparently had the contract with the government to give the physicals. He did not use a stethoscope but put his ear on my shirt and listened to my back and chest. *"C'est bon!* Good!" Then it was Elaine's turn. He asked her to remove her blouse and bra. She looked scared to death. Then he put his ear on her breast and then on her back while pressing on her chest. "C'est bon," he exclaimed! Then he scribbled his signature like all doctors, got his official rubber stamp out of the drawer, hit the ink pad, and stamped the form and said, *"C'est tout,"* that's all. He never bothered to look at Butch or Sandy.

By the end of May, we were airborne for Algeria, where we spent four days with our missionaries, our former landlord, the Seltzers, and our first language teacher, Madame Tavel. We wanted to show off our new three-week-old baby girl. We enjoyed our visit with John and Doris Aseltine and Wilber and Edna Barnes. Our flight to Niamey, Niger, was a night flight on a DC-4. The French airline U.A.T. limited us to twenty kilos of baggage per person, with no baggage allowance for the baby. The airfare for Butch was 50 percent of the adult fare. Sandy's was 10 percent. But the good news was that they didn't weigh our handbags. The French had shopping bags that were nets with a handle. You could bunch them up and stick them in your pocket and they did not take up any more room than a handkerchief. Yet when you put things in them, they expanded. It seemed like there was always room for more, and you could hang them over a finger. Other travelers enjoyed watching missionaries boarding a plane with a child in one arm, while the other hand held three or four net bags almost severing their fingers, with the weight of carrying formula, potty seats, water, diapers, and toys.

Chapter 4.

Arriving in Africa

Go ye therefore, and teach all nations, baptizing in the name of the Father, and of the Son, and of the Holy Ghost.
Matthew 28:19

As the plane descended, our anticipation and excitement soared. It was early morning when our plane touched down on the laterite dirt runway. At last, we were finally in West Africa! As we taxied to the "gate," we left a cloud of orange dust behind us. The airport was nothing more than a little mud building about fifteen-by-twenty feet where we would clear customs and immigration. Bob Richards met us and took us to his home, a rented mud house in the city of Niamey, the capital of the Niger Colony. Niamey only had about twenty thousand souls when we arrived; it now has five hundred thousand. The road was a brand new one-lane black top that stretched four miles from the airport to the edge of the town.

Bob's wife, Carol, had prepared breakfast for us, and we relaxed as we got to know these fine missionaries. After a delightful breakfast and visit, we were taken to the mission station called Yantilla about four kilometers north of town along the banks of the Niger River. Here we were met by Dal and Kay Washer. We stayed in the "Lee house." (They had been missionaries prior to World War II with Christian Missions.) The Lee house was built of mud with a mud roof. The roof was supported by palm logs, which served as joist over which were covered with old fifty-five-gallon gasoline drums that had the top and bottom cut out and then opened and flattened with about six to eight inches of mud that covered them. The roofs, of necessity, were flat, with minimal slope, so the rains would not wash the mud away. They sloped to a round, burned-clay pipe that jetted through the parapet so the water would extend away from the mud walls. The floors were made of rough flag stone. The bathroom had a shower stall but no running water. A fifty-five gallon drum was filled with water by a servant named Gardaba. He was hired by all the missionaries to provide water. He had a donkey, and strapped to the donkey were two five-gallon "tuques" or square tin containers. The tuques had been kerosene containers. Since there was no electricity on the compound, kerosene was used for lamps and to operate refrigerators.

Our baggage, which we had crated back in the States, was shipped to Niger while we were in language study, so I was anxious to locate it and see if the crates were in good condition. It was stored in a mud building, and I was warned to be very careful of snakes. I found it in good condition, other than a few crates had mud tunnels laced across them, which were termite passageways.

While in Paris, we learned that we would be serving in French Sudan, with the town of Gao being our first stop. Dan and Ann Zimmerman, who preceded us to Africa by about sixteen months, had opened up this mission field along the Niger River about four hundred kilometers north of Niamey.

Getting to Gao

Bob Richards made arrangements with a French company in Niamey to transport our freight to Gao. The truck came out to the mission compound and was loaded early one morning, and we were told it would leave within the hour. Bob and I were promised seats next to the driver. Fortunately my six-foot-two-inch body only weighed 150 pounds, and Bob, being shorter, was probably about 135 pounds. So we were fairly comfortable each with a cheek and a half on the seat. About twenty-five locals with their baggage were all loaded on the truck. We kept looking at our watches and watched the hours go by and we had not moved an inch. By now it was 6:00 PM, and it looked like we were about ready to leave. Then we noticed all the passengers who had been sitting on my baggage started to climb down from the truck, each with his little tea pot that had water splashing out of the spout and a small grass mat. It was sunset and prayer time. Each one went through the ceremonial washing of his hands, feet, ears, and private parts and then faced east toward Mecca and began his prayers with exercises. Finally, after about twenty minutes, everybody climbed back and perched high on top of the baggage, and soon the engine was started and we began our four-hundred-kilometer trek in total darkness. Vehicles often were driven at night when it was cooler to prevent engine overheating.

After an hour on the road, in our dim headlights we saw a crocodile crossing the road. The driver deliberately hit it. The collision with the truck killed the crock and gave us a jolt too. Because the meat and hide were valuable, we stopped and loaded the ten-foot crocodile on top of my luggage into the already crowded back of the truck.

We arrived at the town of Tillaberry, where we pulled up on a hill and the driver took a three-hour nap. We had averaged about fifteen to twenty mph. Again it was prayer time, and soon the sun would begin to light the eastern sky. The driver blew his horn, and our passengers completed their breakfasts and slurped down their tea, and we were off again, stopping periodically at puddles to top off the radiator as well as their teapots. The water that they were pouring into the radiator and teapots looked like cocoa, but that did not faze them.

The sandy road was muddy in areas during this the rainy season. Often the French police would close the road for twenty-four hours after a rainstorm, as it seemed there was no bottom to the mud and trucks would make huge ruts and eventually get stuck and buried in the mud.

We traveled all day and into the next night. The border between Niger and the French Sudan was only marked by the rapids in the river. Somewhere between Ansongo and Gao our headlights caught a lion lying in the middle of the road. It got up slowly and went off into the bush. It was the first and last lion I would ever see in the many years I spent in Africa. Today lions no longer exist in northern Mali, as they have been hunted to extinction there. In fact, throughout West Africa, the vast majority of Africans live their entire lifetimes without ever seeing a lion, giraffe, chimpanzee, or other wild animal that people associate with Africa. West African wildlife has disappeared as the forests have been cut, the Sahara desert has expanded south, and the human population has exploded.

Finally, in the middle of the night we arrived in Gao. Gao, the terminus of the Trans-Saharan route coming from Algeria, had a population of about twenty thousand people. The buildings and houses were adobe mud buildings, and most of the city was laid out in blocks with wide streets. The trucking company, Vidal, was located directly across the road from the house where Dan and Ann Zimmerman lived, and thus they were awakened by our noisy truck and all the commotion of the passengers unloading. I did not notice who ended up with the crocodile, but it was probably the chauffer. We were welcomed by the Zimmermans as we sat around a lantern and replayed all the events of the last thirty hours. Soon we could hear the call to prayer coming from various sections of the town as people stirred and began their ritual of the first of five prayer times throughout the day. The sun began to appear in the east, and I got my first glimpse of the town that would be our home for the next six months. Ann prepared us a wonderful breakfast with eggs and something like cream of wheat made from small seeds of grass.

After breakfast, their houseboy, Saidou, arrived. His first chore was to shake out the sand that accumulated in the bedding. During the night, the breeze caused an eddy or whirlpool inside the courtyard where people would be sleeping. People slept outside in the courtyard or on the rooftops because their houses were like mud ovens. Missionaries were advised to pack rollaway beds, which could be folded up during the day and rolled inside the house. So Saidou was busy folding up the beds after divesting them of the sand. Saidou was blacker than I was white, with a shaved round head, a great smile, and gleaming white teeth. He had a sense of balance like no other person I have ever seen. Africans carry most everything on their heads, but Saidou would arrive with an egg on his head and his hands at his side. He could have been rich had he'd been in America just performing what was only natural to him. Had I tried something like that, it would have been scrambled egg disaster.

After devotions and thanking the Lord for a safe trip, we looked for the chauffer. He was hard to find, as some of the passengers stayed by the truck sleeping on their grass mats but completely covered with a sheet or blanket to keep the mosquitoes from them, so the truck was surrounded by what appeared to look like mummies. Which one was the chauffer?

We were anxious to go to the other end of town where Dan had rented a brand-new house for us. By now people were up and around. Many of the townspeople were on their way to the market. Finally the driver was identified, and he started up the truck, startling the people sleeping under it. They scrambled away, and we were off to the north side of the town.

The house that Dan had rented for us belonged to Jean Marou, the director of a school and the son-in-law of the first missionary to Timbuktu, a Catholic priest who had married a Songhai woman. We were very pleased with the house. It had three rooms and a veranda, plus a storeroom separate from the house. It had a nice yard where Butch could play. We unloaded everything into the house and storeroom and locked them up.

The next thing on our mind was to find transportation back to Niamey. We caught the weekly bus between Gao and Niamey. The bus was a combination truck-bus. The front half had seats, and the back half was truck. About ninety kilometers from Gao, we were rolling along at a pretty good clip when all of a sudden we hit into deep, loose sand and we jolted to an abrupt stop. We sat on an angle and discovered that the back wheels of the truck had been torn off of the body of the bus! Yes, the wheels, axle, springs, and differential were all pretty much intact but lying on the sand about thirty feet behind us! We realized that we were helpless. But God knew our problem, and the *hand of the Lord* would again be displayed.

After sitting in the shade of the truck for about an hour, we heard the sound of a truck on the road. Could it be that there would be room for us and it was heading to Niamey? Would it be able to get around the wheels and what was left of the bus on this one-track, miserable path? All of the trucks carried, tied to the sides of their vehicles, two steel runners about sixteen feet long that were made for building airplane runways during WWII. As the truck approached, it too got stuck in the sand, but with the steel tracks and all of its passengers pushing, it finally got to a mud flat. The driver and owner of this pre-WWII Citroen truck was none other than Paul, a Nigerian who attended the church that Bob Richards pastored in Niamey. Wow, the Lord knew exactly where we were and put the right people in the right place at the right time to take care of us. These were great experiences that helped us have a greater appreciation for the conditions and circumstances that the people to which God had called us to minister faced.

Now Paul's truck was not a Cadillac. In fact, in the States, it would not have been welcomed in a junkyard! We made many stops as the steam blew out from under the hood. We had to be "spotters" looking for puddles to refresh the boiling radiator. The muddy water that was poured into the radiator seemed to plug up the leaks. Then there were the stops to take off the carburetor to clean it, blow on it, and suck out the dirt from the plugged holes, but after about twenty-four hours, we were back at the mission compound at Yantilla for a glorious reunion with Elaine, Butch, and Sandy, who was now two months old. There were no crocodiles or lions in our trip back home, but we did see hundreds of wild Guinea fowl, which we would learn taste just like chicken!

Now with all of our baggage (beds, table, dressers, kitchen utensils, etc.) safely in Gao, the next thing on the agenda was to get the family to Gao. Knowing what we had just been through getting our baggage to Gao, I was not looking forward to putting Elaine, Butch, and two-month-old Sandy through more experiences like I'd just survived. But again the *hand of the Lord* became very evident. Bob Richards told us the French army had a flight every other week that took supplies to the army base in Gao. When there was room and the weight limit would allow, they would take women and children from the French military or colonial administrators. He inquired and found that they would have room for us. Wow, what a relief!

The airplane was an old German World War II Junker. What an appropriate name! It was a tri-motor, and the body was corrugated metal. Out on the wings on each side was a glass tube with a floater in it that told you how much gasoline you had in the tanks in the wings. A couple of French soldiers joined us on board. Each engine was revved up individually, and we sat on pull-down seats facing each other with our seatbelts securely fastened and holding Sandy on my lap. Then with all three engines at full power, we put a cloud of dust in the cloudless sky as we vibrated down the dirt runway and became airborne. The noise made it impossible to converse, and soon we were cruising at about 145 mph. The plane did not have any finished interior nor air vents, just the bare metal skin over the riveted ribs, but to our surprise, we watched a French soldier roll down a window about two inches, and we finally had some circulation of air as the sun heated up what seemed like a big can. After about an hour and a half, we approached the airport at Gao, another laterite dirt strip. Upon landing, we learned that a French commercial aircraft had crashed there a month earlier, killing all on board.

We were met at the airport by Dan Zimmerman and Captain Helmling. Captain Helmling was the commander of the army base in Gao. He and his wife were Protestants and attended the Sunday morning services that the Zimmemans had in a small building in the courtyard of their rented house. The Zimmermans did not have a vehicle, but Captain Helmling had use of an old WWII army truck.

It was early July 1952 when we arrived in Gao, and our first priority was to get our freight unpacked, especially our beds and crib, so we could sleep. A large metal (everything had to be metal because of the termites) armoire had been packed full of bedding and other supplies. Our house had three rooms and a veranda, a bedroom, a kitchen, and a dining room. The veranda served as a living area. Our cooking was done on a small kerosene space heater in a four-quart pressure cooker. Another priority was to take some of the boards from our crates and saw them to make frames for screens. It was the rainy season and mosquito season. Clothes lines were strung to tie up mosquito nets outside in the courtyard were we slept under the stars.

The next five months were spent studying the Gao dialect of the Songhai language. Dan Zimmerman was our language teacher. He was quite a linguist, and in just a year, he had learned more than I did in the next twenty years. The Africans used to say he could correct them in the usage of their own language.

On July 14, we went to the main road to view the Bastille parade put on by the military. It was very interesting and consisted of both French and African soldiers. They were on foot and a few vehicles, but the most interesting were the camel corps of about one hundred camels with French and Nomadic soldiers riding high on their saddles, which bridged these one humped dromedaries. They were dressed in white robes (called *boubous*) with indigo sashes and turbans partially veiled. Each was armed with a rifle. This part of the military patrolled the desert and the caravan routes and appeared in town about once a month to load up their camels with food and other provisions. They were an elite corps of desert troops. They learned to live in the desert like the nomads. Their food was cooked over a fire made up of dried camel dung. In the desert, it took less than a day to dry the dung. These men were true warriors, as the French and Tuareg nomads had been at war only a few years earlier. Whenever a diplomat or government official would come to town, hundreds of these soldiers on camels would come in from the desert to join a welcoming parade.

I had shipped my motorcycle to Niamey from Paris. The airline had a special subsidized rate for passengers to ship their personal effects. We depended on our little two-cycle Peuget for transportation around Gao. The main market and the Zimmermans' house were both about two kilometers from our house. I made two large saddle bags out of a large, heavy-duty canvas trunk that fit on the sides of the back wheel. These were large enough to carry a five-gallon jerry can in each one. The rack over the rear wheel was fitted with a passenger seat with two pedals to rest your feet on. We were a family of four. I sat on the driver's seat, Elaine was perched on the passenger's seat, and Butch straddled the gas tank and sat in front of me. Sandy was carried in Elaine's arms. We were the only motorcycle gang in town, and the Africans called our vehicle "pucka–pucka," which resembled the sound of the motor. Elaine learned to handle the cycle well as she would go to the Zimmermans for a language lesson while I babysat Sandy. We alternated taking lessons. She had to look for a wall to come alongside of when she wanted to stop, as even though the cycle was small, she could not handle or balance it when she stopped.

Upon our arrival in Gao, we met the man who was undoubtedly the first Songhai convert and for many years the only Songhai Christian. His name was Attino. We came to know and love him. Attino (meaning Monday, because probably he was born on Monday) who was a vibrant believer who had been saved through the witness of a missionary couple with Christian and Missionary Alliance (C&MA) prior to WWII. (After the war, the C&MA turned their area in Gao and Timbuktu over to our organization, Christian Missions, since our missionaries were working with the same language group in Niger—the Zarma dialect.) Attino was faithful, along with his wife and children, at all of the services in the little chapel in the yard at the Zimmermans' home. After coming to Christ in the mid-1930s, Attino went to Bible school at N'Torroso about one thousand kilometers from Gao. The school was taught in the Bambara language, which meant he had to learn to read, write, and speak the Bambara language. N'Torroso was in an animistic area of French Sudan and was not influenced by the Muslims of the north. Upon completing Bible school, he ministered as an evangelist and then later returned to his home in Gao, where he would encounter and endure tremendous persecution from the fanatic Muslims. Imagine living in a city of twenty thousand and you are the only Christian! But he was vocal and never attempted to hide his faith. He supported his family as a tailor. Clothing was not sold in the stores or marketplace but rather material was sold by the *coubre* (tip of the finger to the elbow) and then taken to a tailor to be sewed. He had been provided a treadle sewing machine, and his honesty and integrity brought him many clients from the Muslim community. He would later manage the Christian bookstore operated by our Mission.

PRE-TIMBUKTU

David at six months

David as a young sailor 1945-1946

David and Elaine Marshall eight days after their wedding day June 12, 1948

*Wilber and Edna Barnes and David and Elaine with the founder of
the mission, Joe McCaba at the sailing on December 2, 1950*

At sea going to Mali for our second term, David, Sandy and Diane, 1956

Our freight being loaded for a trip to Gao in June 1952

Our flight to Gao in a German Junker

Desert soldiers on parade in Gao, July 14, 1952

Dan Zimmerman and evangelist Attino Maiga using a dugout canoe to visit villages along the Niger River

The riverboat General Soumare docked along the Niger River

Narrow gauge train leaving Dakar for Bamako

David giving his brother Frank a hair cut

Chapter 5.

To Timbuktu

But ye shall receive power, after that the Holy Ghost is come upon you: and ye shall be witnesses unto me both in Jerusalem, and in all Judea, and in Samaria, and unto the uttermost part of the earth. Acts 1:8

By now we decided to move upriver four hundred kilometers to the ancient city of Timbuktu. We received permission from our field counsel but needed permission from the French to move there with young children. They did not allow French families to live there if they had children under the age of two because so many children died there from dehydration. However, we received permission, with the condition that we followed certain rules such as having screens to keep the flies and mosquitoes out. We were going to serve our Lord in Timbuktu!

A Bit of Background

Many children first encounter the name while reading the popular children's book, *From Kalamazoo to Timbuktu*. Even many adults are surprised to learn that such a place actually exists. This city has intrigued outsiders for centuries.

Considering the romance surrounding the name, the word Timbuktu has an unlikely meaning. The story behind the name begins in the year 1080, when Nomadic herders set up camp along the north bank of the Niger at the present location of Timbuktu. During the rainy season, they went north to graze their livestock, leaving their belongings and the young and elderly of their clan in the care of a woman named Bouctou ("woman with the large navel"). *Tin*, meaning "place of," was added to the woman's name, and the settlement became known as Tin-Bouctou—"place of the woman with the large navel." Over the centuries, the English rendering took the form Timbuktu.

Because of its strategic location at the southern edge of the desert and at the northernmost point in the arc formed by the Niger River, the settlement became the place where "the camel met the canoe." Camel caravans brought salt, silk, spices, copper, and tea from regions to the north and east. These were traded for gold, ivory, kola nuts, ostrich feathers, and slaves, all of which were brought up from the south by boat. The salt was particularly valuable, at one time being traded for gold pound for pound. It was in Timbuktu that these cargos were unloaded, exchanged, and then reloaded on the camels and canoes and sent on their way to distant markets. (Even to this day, Timbuktu's economy is based on trade.)

The city experienced fabulous growth, becoming a bustling commercial center. However, Tuareg herders controlled the town and levied enormous taxes on the wealthy merchants and traders. Finally, at the request of the citizens, the great Malian Emperor Kankan Moussa liberated the city from the Tuaregs in the early 1300s.

The wealth of the Malian empire was unsurpassed at this period in history. In 1323, Kankan Moussa began a pilgrimage to Mecca. He passed through Timbuktu with an entourage of sixty thousand people, including twelve thousand slaves attired in silks and rich fabrics. Five hundred slaves preceded him, each carrying a gold staff weighing six pounds. Moussa rode on horseback, followed by eighty camels each carrying three hundred pounds in gold dust. Moussa bestowed large amounts of gold in the holy cities of Medina and Mecca, as well as in Cairo. While passing through Cairo, Moussa gave away so much that the price of gold and the value of the Egyptian currency slumped for several years. According to one Islamic historian, the price did not recover for twelve years. Along the journey, wherever he stopped to pray each Friday, he had a mosque built. On his return trip in 1325, Moussa again passed through Timbuktu. He ordered that a mosque be built by a famous Moorish poet and architect from Granada named Es-Saheli. This mosque is still used. The city prospered until the fifteenth century, when it slipped back into Tuareg control.

In the sixteenth century, Timbuktu became part of the Songhai Empire, and it again flourished. The city was renowned throughout the Islamic world. Two universities were established, one of which specialized in law and theology had an enrollment of twenty-five hundred students. Another twenty-five thousand students studied in the 180 Koranic schools.

At least twenty-five tailors annually trained fifty to one hundred apprentices each. The government subsidized doctors, scholars, and judges. Poets and philosophers exiled from Spain took refuge in Timbuktu, bringing with them literary treasures and contributing to the creation of a scholarly and erudite society. The population grew to one hundred thousand. Each year, tens of thousands of camels unloaded their freight in the city. Gold flowed freely, much of it forming the basis of European economies. Rumors and sketchy reports of a stunning royal court and a city roofed with gold found their way back to Europe.

In 1591, Berbers from Morocco, using firearms for the first time in the region, invaded and conquered Timbuktu. This was the beginning of Timbuktu's demise. They executed the scholars, and camel caravans carried away Timbuktu's legendary riches. Throughout the seventeenth and eighteenth centuries, the city was attacked and pillaged time and time again, until there was little left worth fighting for. In the end, the strategic location that brought prosperity to the city brought its fall, as the site was coveted by all those seeking to control the region.

Europeans, unaware of the city's decline, continued to be captivated with stories of its wealth. Between the 1500s and 1853, at least forty-three Europeans attempted to reach Timbuktu, of whom only four succeeded. During this time, going to Timbuktu came to mean "going to the ends of the earth." In 1824, the Geographical Society of Paris offered a reward of ten thousand francs for the first explorer to return with a verifiable account of the city. A Scot named Gordon Laing reached the city in 1826. However, upon hearing that a Christian had arrived in the city, the sultan who claimed control of the town ordered him to leave or be put to death. Laing left, but he and most of his servants were killed during the night about thirty miles outside of Timbuktu. One of his servants escaped and arrived back in Tripoli two years later with a copy of Laing's notes.

Rene Caille, a Frenchman, was the first European to make it to Timbuktu and return alive. Before attempting the trip, he lived in North Africa, learning Arabic and immersing himself in Muslim culture. He then headed off alone, disguised as an Egyptian. After many brushes with death, he finally arrived in Timbuktu on April 20, 1828. Caille wrote about his first impressions, "I looked around and found that the sight before me did not answer my expectations. I had formed an entirely different idea of the grandeur and wealth of Timbuktu." He stayed only two weeks before joining a camel caravan heading north across the desert to Tangiers, the first of many disappointed visitors. From there he returned to Europe with an accurate account of what little remained of the city.

In the 1880s, the European presence in the area became permanent as the French came to conquer and colonize. Mali became a French colony in 1883, although Timbuktu was not conquered until 1893.

We would not be the first missionaries to be sent to this ancient but spiritually needy city. Christian and Mission Alliance (C&MA) sent a whole group of missionaries (about fifteen families) to Timbuktu from Sierra Leone. Most died within the first year as they traveled up the Niger River. The first missionaries to become established in Timbuktu were the Kurlacks. They arrived in 1928, but the wife died after only a few years there. In fact, we took care of her grave during the time we lived in Timbuktu. Then a French Canadian missionary arrived named Sauve', who also died shortly after his arrival. Truly, you can see why West Africa was called "White Man's Grave." The next missionary was Floyd Bowman and his wife. They came in 1936 and were the first to work with the Tuaregs. He translated the gospel of Matthew into Tamasheq. Years later, I found a convert from the Bowmans' work living about 150 kilometers downriver.

Timeless Timbuktu

What is Timbuktu like? In many ways it is a town where time stands still. It is much the same today as it was when we moved there. Timbuktu is a small (population about fifteen thousand) town with few signs of its glorious and proud past. The town is bleached pale brown. During most of the year, its jagged outlines are sharply contrasted with a blinding desert blue sky. The dry, mud brick buildings blend into the landscape as if they were intended to be camouflaged. During the dry, windy harmattan season, the air is thick with dust and sand as the Sahara becomes airborne. Gone is the glare of the sun reflecting off of the sand, the crisp, black shadows, and azure sky. The brown city is enveloped by the brown sky.

Driving into town, visitors pass scattered, squat, beleaguered-looking acacia trees, each seemingly with a goat attached. Standing on their hind legs, goats browse the plant into submission, as if shaping a bonsai. Ubiquitous children and roaming merchants swarm around vehicles before visitors have a chance to get sand in their shoes. All of them are wanting the same thing—money. The merchants are willing to part with Tuareg swords, knives, camel whips, or teapots if the price is right, whereas the children merely seek a *cadeau* (a gift).

Whereas Americans think of Timbuktu as a place that is remote, a place at the end of the earth, the French think of Timbuktu as a mysterious city. Tourism posters entice intrepid travelers to seek out "Mysterious Timbuktu." Because of all of the men just loitering around the street corners all day and sitting in the shade of scattered trees, Madame LeBoydeck often said the mystery of Timbuktu is that, "Everybody eats, but nobody works." This is the way it appeared—men just sitting in the market with their sticks talking among themselves. Over the years, many tourists have wondered what exactly was the mystery of Timbuktu. A Malian minister of sport, art, and culture was once asked what made Timbuktu mysterious. He replied, "If I told you why it is mysterious then it would not be mysterious." Maybe he was right. It is the mystery that is a mystery. But to many visitors the most profound mysteries upon arrival are, "What am I doing in this hot, dusty, fly-infested place?" and "What am I going to do now that I'm here?"

Flies are a terrible problem in Timbuktu. They coat clothes and crawl over the people's faces. Children and babies who don't brush them off have flies crawling in their mouths, nostrils, and ears. People coming into church would carry dozens of flies on the back of their robes and dresses. It was not unusual for flies to get into our mouths as we sang hymns. About once a month, as I would be enthusiastically singing I would swallow one as I would be taking a big breath when it entered my mouth.

Donkeys, although less annoying than flies, are also abundant in Timbuktu. They are used to carry freight on their backs and sometimes to pull water up out of wells. On one occasion, the French conducted a census of Timbuktu and counted eight thousand people and eight thousand donkeys!

Although Timbuktu often does not live up to its advanced billing, a visit may still be rewarding if one takes the time to stroll through the narrow, crooked streets and absorb life in the Sahel. This unassuming town, seemingly oblivious to its worldwide recognition, has a certain humble charm. Throughout the town, women bake bread in dome-shaped ovens made of clay and as tall as the women using them. They skillfully extract the round loaves out of the fire with a long-handled spade and then drop the bread onto the sand to cool. The bread, called *takoula*, is much like the bread used in the middle east and probably resembles the five loaves that the boy gave to Jesus. In recent years, it has become popular in the United States, and we call it "pocket bread." Many modest, simple mud homes have enormous wooden doors with ornate metal work on them.

These curious "Doors of Timbuktu" may be relics from the Moroccan invasion of the fifteenth century.

The streets in Timbuktu are basically narrow alleyways. They twist and turn through mud buildings, so that it is impossible to give directions. To walk the sand streets of Timbuktu is to walk through a living nativity scene: shepherds watching their flocks as they meander through the narrow, winding streets; camels, donkeys, and wise men in ornate brightly colored robes; and Tuareg men and women with somber blue robes and covered heads, looking like every Mary and Joseph in every manger scene. And at Christmas there is no room in the inn as tourists, mostly French, come to escape winter and get their passports stamped "TOMBOUCTOU." Looking at the city from the dunes outside of town also presents a Christmas card scene—the generic silhouette of Bethlehem, complete with camels in the foreground and a brilliant desert sky with the evening star suspended over the city.

The people of Timbuktu were predominately a tribe or people called Songhai, and they have their own language called Songhai. This is the main language used in the market and follows along the Niger River for over one thousand miles with various dialects. Around the edges of town were nomadic Tuaregs who would occasionally come into town, especially in times of drought and famine. They lived in huts made from sticks and covered with grass mats and animal hides. The grass was transported on camel backs from some areas in the desert where adequate rainfall produced tall grass. Some also grew wheat and used the straw to make thatch. The "homes" were built by the women, even elderly women, to honor their husbands

For centuries, and still today, much of the trade is centered around salt. The Moors mined salt nearly one thousand kilometers (six hundred miles) north of Timbuktu in the middle of the Sahara and transported most of it to Timbuktu, where it was sold to the Songhai traders. The salt was mined in bars about forty inches long, fifteen to nineteen inches wide, and about two inches thick. This was transported by camel, each camel carrying four bars weighing about sixty-five to seventy pounds per bar. The camels came in groups, but the entire ensemble consisted of about ten thousand. They came twice a year, and it took about a month for all of them to arrive. Three or four men led each group. It seemed like those men walked most of the way. They were short in stature, and it appeared they had walked their legs off. They were ambitious and hard working, as they were responsible to unload the salt at Timbuktu, and often they unloaded the salt along the caravan route to rest their camels.

Most mud houses in Timbuktu were two stories, and the salt was stored in rooms on the ground floor. Some salt was consumed in Timbuktu and the surrounding areas, but most of it was loaded into very large canoes and paddled or poled four hundred kilometers up river to Mopti, where there was a huge market and a road that would extend their market all the way to the coast. All over West Africa you will find salt that at one time was in the hands of Timbuktu people. The main diet of the people in northern Mali is rice and millet. But unfortunately, north of Mopti not enough is grown, and the population is dependent on the people in the south for their food. Thus, salt is bartered for grain, and both the businesspeople of Timbuktu and the businesspeople in the south know how to play the game. The people in the north keep the salt in storerooms in their houses until the people in the south are desperate for salt and the price goes up. On the other hand, people in the north are facing famine, and this drives the price up, as the people are hungry and will pay a higher price. The French government tried hard to fix prices by buying up huge amounts of grain and setting the price and rationing it out by fixed amounts per month, thus controlling the price and also the famine. This helped somewhat, but there was still a large black market. They were dealing with very experienced businesspeople.

Another important market for salt was that in the south, part of the dowry for buying a wife included several bars of salt. When you think about it, a wife was usually given in marriage at the age of twelve or thirteen, and in an Islamic culture, a man could have as many as four wives, which meant that thousands of bars of salt were paid each month for dowries. The girl was expected to have a child within a year, or else the husband would think, "She isn't worth her salt," and he would marry another.

Making Our Move

Before moving the family to Timbuktu, I thought about trying to make an exploratory trip on my motorcycle, but on the advice of Dan, we decided we would go together to the town of Bourem about ninety-five kilometers north of Gao. Bourem was less than one-fourth of the way and was where the Niger River made its big bend and began flowing south. We set out early in the morning. Dan was on the back seat, and things went pretty well for about a half an hour, but then we got into a lot of sand. Dan jumped off the back and began pushing while I gunned the motor and shifted to low gear. This happened very frequently, and a few times we both got off and pushed. We finally arrived in Bourem and went to an old fort built high on a hill with a beautiful view of the river and the "road" going north to Algeria. We were exhausted.

The fort had been made into a *campement* for weary travelers. A *campement* was more than a campground, but not quite a hotel. It would be a bed and roof over your head, but without running water or flush toilets. A guard served as a cook. He heated up a can of cassoulet (French baked beans) that I liked much better than American baked beans. To our surprise, the French military were on maneuvers, and Captain Helming appeared "out of the blue." They were heading back to their base at Gao, and he offered to take us home. It didn't take much coaxing and we loaded our "pucka-pucka" in the back of his four-wheel-drive army vehicle and after a couple of hours and numerous sand pits, we arrived back in Gao. That convinced me not try to go to Timbuktu on my cycle. There is no way that I could have made it, as the three hundred kilometers between Bourem and Timbuktu could not even be called a road. In fact, it would have been unusual to have more than one or two vehicles a month take this stretch of loose, powdery sand, and within an hour their tracks would be made to disappear by the nearly constant wind.

In late November, Dan and I boarded a small riverboat called the *Bonnier* and headed for Koriome, the port for Timbuktu located seven kilometers south of town. The accommodations were not the best, but it was better than going on the cycle and certainly a lot safer. The trip included stops at Bourem, Gourma Rharous, and then Koriome. Each stop was exciting, as scores of passengers and tons of freight were loaded and unloaded. The freight going upstream was minimal and consisted mostly of large rolls of grass mats, which were used as beds and roof coverings in the construction of houses. The grass mats also were made into sacks for grain, charcoal, and cotton. Bourem exported *terre de Bourem* which was a yellowish clay or shale that was used in other towns. This was crushed in a mortar by a pestle into a fine powder and mixed with some Arabic gum and karate butter and cooked in a large pot or steel drum, and then it was plastered on the outside of buildings, especially the east side of the building, to protect the mud bricks from the rain, as storms generally came from the east. Sacks of grain generally weighed 100 kilos or 220 pounds. These were carried on and off the boat on the backs of laborers, generally Bellas, who were considered the slave race. In fact, the word Bella means slave. These men were very muscular and did most of the hard labor. Most of these men were no longer slaves, but slavery did still exist in the area.

Our next problem was traveling the last seven kilometers to Timbuktu. Fortunately a Frenchmen met the boat and had an old army vehicle. He managed a French store in town called Morel et Prom. He was kind enough to take us on the sandy road into town while the freight was loaded onto the backs of donkeys, which formed a caravan between Timbuktu and Koriome. We were dropped off at the *Campment,* which served as the hotel in Timbuktu. There we met quite a mix of people, including an Englishmen who was a student at Oxford and an older French couple who kept us entertained by telling us stories about being in Somalia during the war and how they became so desperate for food that they resorted to being cannibals and eating human flesh. Another Belgian couple was trying to hitch a ride across the great Sahara, and then there was Madame LeBoydeck, who weighed in at about four hundred pounds. She was there with her nineteen-year-old daughter, who I estimated was close to three hundred pounds. They had just arrived, and their goal was to collect wild animals that they planned to take back to France and Belgium to sell to zoos and circuses. Madame let us know that she would be in charge, as she did not trust the cook, indicating that the Muslim cook might try to poison us. (I think she was afraid that he would not cook enough to satisfy her appetite.) Of course, the *campement* had no running water or bathroom facilities, but there was an enclosure about fifty feet away with some cheap clay pots. The guard's job description included emptying the pots in the "potter's field" when needed.

We listened to these incredible stories as we sat around the table eating the meal that Madame had prepared for us. She pushed what must have been at least two pounds of meat onto my plate. Not only was it an enormous amount to eat, but it was as tough as leather! By now I had actually grown another inch since I arrived in Africa but was still a skinny 150 lbs at six-foot-three. I think she wanted to fatten me up, maybe for the cannibal that was sharing the room next to us. This was my first night in Timbuktu, the town we'd call home for more than twenty years.

Home Hunting

The next morning, we set out early to tour the town and see what might be available to rent. It didn't take long for word to spread in town that the two lanky guys who had invaded their town were Americans looking for a house to rent. We quickly met a roly-poly-shaped man with a big smile. He said he had a house for rent and beckoned us to follow him. He led us down a narrow road that emptied into a small open-air marketplace called *yobou tao* or new market. The road to the market was lined with "souks" or small Arab shops selling tea, cloth, small tea glasses, loafs of sugar from Morocco, and brass serving platters used for ceremonial tea. Across from the market was a two-story mud house with an impressive front door characteristic of Timbuktu. He took a large key from his pocket and opened the door.

There were no windows on the ground floor. We stepped across the threshold onto the sand floor. Directly in front of us was a large pillar that supported the palm logs, which acted as joist for the second floor. Across the palm logs were sticks laid side by side, which were then covered with woven grass mats, and on top of this was a covering of about six inches of mud, which accounted for the second floor. There were two rooms each, with a large mud brick pillar in the center. The second room had a four-by-six-foot opening that opened to the roof, giving light to that room. From the first room a stairway led to a veranda on the second floor. The second floor consisted of a large room again with a pillar in the middle supporting the mud roof. Off of this main room were two small rooms about six feet wide, one about nine feet long and the other about five feet long. A covered veranda about eight feet wide ran the width of the house. The house was brand new and had only been used once when all of the thirteen-year-old boys in the town were locked in for a few days while they went through the ritual and celebration performed by the Imams of circumcision. I couldn't help thinking about Genesis 17:25 when Ishmael was circumcised. The surgeries were done with crude knives, but most seem to survive. Most importantly, the property had a large additional storeroom, which could be made into a store, as it would open up on the marketplace.

We agreed to pay the equivalent of $35 per month for the house and an additional $15 per month for the storeroom at the back. Our support level by this time had risen to $150 per month, so this would leave us with $100 for our family of four. We then negotiated to have the mud walls white washed and the mud steps replaced with alhor, a soft white stone that was mined in the desert. We also arranged with a carpenter to build frames between the openings between the pillars on the back veranda so we could screen in our bedrooms, which were on the second floor. Butch would have the larger of the small rooms, and Elaine and I would have the large room with the crib for Sandy. We also negotiated with the mason to put a thin coat of cement over the mud bedroom floors and the veranda. We hoped it would be ready for us to move in by December 20, 1952.

Before leaving, Dan and I visited the FAO store in town, which was a large chain all over French West Africa. They sold flour, sugar, and cloth, as well as gasoline and kerosene. The gasoline and kerosene were shipped in fifty-five-gallon drums. Although smaller merchants sold by the liter, we bought gasoline and kerosene by the drums.

While we were in the FAO store, we were accosted by a tall, thin man who spoke excellent French, and he introduced himself as the "pastor" in Timbuktu. He began to quote Scripture to us and it soon became apparent that he was extremely intelligent, but also that he was crazy. We learned he used to be a schoolteacher and at one time ran for a political office, but at some point he was introduced to alcohol, which totally ruined his mind and his behavior. When he quoted Scripture, he would tell you what translation he was quoting from as well as the date it was published. He would go to the doctor and recite from memory from medical texts, and then he would go to the radio station technician and recite from memory from electronics textbooks. He had a photographic memory.

After moving to Timbuktu, we eventually got to know this amazing man, Abdoulai. I will never forget one conversation I had with him outside my gate. The night before a Malian Independence Day in the mid-1960s, electricity was first switched on in Timbuktu. We even had street lights for the first time ever. The next morning, I heard Abdoulai at my gate, and I went out to greet him. He said, "Pastor, can you make my voice be heard at the United Nations?"

I said, "Probably not, but what's the problem?"

He said, "These lights are crazy. They must turn them off. The world must know this! We cannot afford to feed our children and to clothe them properly. And we sleep out in the streets at night and now they turn the lights on us so we cannot sleep. They are wasting money!"

Well, Mr. Abdoulai was quite correct in his assessment of having street lights in this impoverished town. Dan Zimmerman then came out of the house to join the conversation, and he greeted Abdoulai by saying, "Happy Independence Day!" And with great wisdom and sincerity, this so-called crazy man said to Dan, "Pastor, nobody is independent but God."

Dan and I returned to Gao by boat, and by December 20, the family and I were aboard the *Mage*, a two-deck riverboat. The *Mage* originally was a paddle wheel boat run by steam; however, there was no wood for fuel in this area, so it was pulled by a diesel engine tugboat. We had two cabins on the second deck. Elaine had one with Sandy, and I shared the other with Butch. From the second deck, we could look at the scenery along the shore. In one spot, we saw hippos on the end of a small island eating the tall river grass.

Even more interesting than the wildlife were the other people on the boat. Perhaps the best way to study culture is to take a riverboat excursion of several days or go on a large canoe trip of several days. We could look down on the front of the boat where the crew's wives lived with their children. They had open fires where they cooked their meals on top of a three-pronged piece of pottery; between each prong was a piece of wood, which came from more than one thousand kilometers south where there were still forests remaining. On top of the three prongs was a clay pot with boiling water, containing several pieces of dried fish, which had first been knocked together to dislodge some of the maggots and the flies that had covered it prior to being put in the pot. Just as onshore, the air was filled with the constant rhythmic sound of thumping of the large wooden pestles pounding the grain in the large wooden mortars. The grain was periodically dumped from the mortar onto a round woven grass tray, and from the tray it was flipped into the air where the wind would blow away the chaff. Then from about six feet it was poured back into the mortar for additional pounding. The process was repeated several times, and finally after a thorough cleaning, it was poured into the cooked fish and cooked for an hour or so.

A bucket with a rope tied to the handle would be dropped overboard for water. The women would bathe their naked children on the deck, pouring water over them. The older kids loved it, just like our kids enjoyed a cool shower, but this was the cool season, and the breeze blowing across the deck was cold. It was also the time of the year when the younger children would catch cold, especially the babies. Just as an example of how Africa is another world compared to what we are used to, mothers would suck the mucus from their baby's nostrils. (I will spare the reader the description of how mothers on the boat gave their babies daily enemas.) These are very clean people, but the perception of certain activities is much different than ours. Later when we opened our bookstore, our women customers would come in with their money rolled up and put up into their noses for lack of a better place to carry it. Of course, when they purchased something, they would pull the money out their nose and hand us the end that had been inserted. Likewise, men would carry their coins in their mouths and then spit them into your hand to make a transaction. People didn't like coins there; when they dropped a coin in the loose sand, it often meant the coin was lost for good or involved much sifting through the sand, hence they put them in their mouths. Money needed to be laundered in Timbuktu! The practices were more fascinating than disgusting. It was just all of part of the culture.

I learned other things on the riverboat. On the top deck of the riverboat, there was a wonderful restaurant serving fancy French food. I especially loved the deviled eggs with elaborate designs on top made with the mayonnaise. You would have thought you were in a high-class restaurant in Paris. One day I went down to the lower decks where they prepared the food and watched the chef working. To make the mayonnaise, he would have to beat egg yolks vigorously. And while beating the egg yolks, he would have to put a drop of peanut oil into the mixture one drop at a time. In Paris, they would have had a kitchen device to add drops of oil, but here the chef took a swig of the peanut oil and then as needed, he would spit one drop of oil at a time into the batter. Those fancy deviled eggs were less appealing after I witnessed the making of the home-made mayonnaise.

Once while traveling on the riverboat coming up from Mopti to Timubktu we had a memorable lesson in water quality. It was an extremely hot day and the river contributed to the humidity. Elaine and I were wet with perspiration when we entered the air conditioned dining room. As we sat at our table our backs felt a chill as they touched the cool chairs. The table was set with a table cloth and cloth napkins. The waiter came with a small fancy bucket of ice and with a set of prongs put cubes of ice in our glasses. In the middle of the table was a carafe of water which was somewhat cloudy, but not too bad considering that the Niger River functions as a sewer for thousands of people and livestock living along the river. The waiter had gone to another table so I looked more carefully at the water and discovered a tiny fish swimming in a circular fashion round and round in the carafe. I was thirsty and wanted to fill our glasses before our ice cubes would melt but I stopped short of shocking the baby fish on the ice cubes. I called to the waiter who was dressed smartly in his starched white jacket. He came immediately with a big smile and said, "Monsieur, how can I help you? "Is the water filtered," I asked. "*Bien sur*"(for certain) monsieur, all of our water is filtered. I picked up the carafe and showed him the fish swimming around in the carafe aquarium. His handsome black face seemed to turn red with embarrassment as he took my drinking water and poured it overboard. He disappeared and within a few minutes he returned with a fresh bottle or carafe of water. He was gone just long enough to get the bucket in the kitchen with the rope tied on the handle and throw it into the river and dip enough to refill the carafe. As he put it back on the table with a big smile his teeth gleaning. I did not want to embarrass him in front of the other first class passengers, so I just returned his smile.

Chapter 6.
Our Life in Timbuktu

"Never pity missionaries; envy them. They are where the real action is -- where life and death, sin and grace, Heaven and Hell converge." Robert C. Shannon

We arrived at Koriome, the port for Timbuktu, about noon on December 22. We were fortunate to get a ride to the *campement* in an old WWII open vehicle owned by the manager of the Morel & Prom store, one of three stores in Timbuktu owned and operated by French companies. This was the only privately owned vehicle in town. At this time, transportation between the river and Timbuktu was done on the backs of donkeys or camels. Timbuktu was four miles (seven kilometers) from Koriome. Unlike my last stay there, only a couple of weary travelers were at the *campement*. Since we had last been there, Madam LeBoydek and her daughter had rented a house with a small courtyard just across the marketplace from where we had rented our house. She had cages with one adult lion and four lion cubs, crocodiles, gazelle, several ostriches, and other birds. Eventually she rented a barge and took all of her animals down river to ship to Europe. Although a bit eccentric, she and her nineteen-year-old daughter became friends of ours and helped us get settled.

Approximately one hundred Frenchmen lived in the town at this time. This included the postmaster and his wife, a judge, a veterinarian, a civil commander, and two managers of the three French stores. The rest were French military. Several hundred colonial soldiers, most of which were Africans from other French colonies, also were stationed in Timbuktu.

The only truck in town, a small dump truck, could be rented with its driver from the government agency called the *Prevoyance*. This agency purchased and stored grain, mainly rice and millet, to ensure a food supply for the long dry season and when the city was isolated because the river being too shallow for shipping. We arranged with this organization to transport our baggage from the port to our newly rented house. By Christmas Eve, we were moved in with all of our baggage sprawled around in our house in Timbuktu.

Home Sweet Home

We set up our wood stove as soon as we could get a chimney built and made room for a fifty-five-gallon drum of water and two cases stacked on top of each other to store pots and pans and other utensils. I buried three fifty-five-gallon drums under the sand floor, which would serve as a septic tank for the toilet and shower upstairs. I hand chiseled a four-inch hole in the sides of the barrels and connected them together with empty powdered milk cans. The brand name was KLIM—milk spelled backwards. The tops were clamped on each barrel, and the first barrel lid also had a four-inch hole chiseled in it so the sewage from upstairs would drain into it. The pipe from upstairs to the barrel downstairs was made from several burnt clay pipes cemented together and then encased with mud bricks. The first barrel held the raw sewage. This overflowed via a milk can into the second barrel, which was filled with charcoal that was available in the market. This allowed the fluids to flow through it to the bottom of the barrel, where it connected to the third barrel through another milk can. This barrel was also filled with charcoal, so the fluids were also filtered as they rose to the top. Near the top of the third barrel, the last four-inch hole was cut to allow what was supposed to be filtered sewage and would exit them through clay pipes to the outside of the house to a barrel I had buried in the street. I had punctured holes in this barrel so that when the sewer water drained into the barrel, it would drain into the sand under the ground. Surprisingly, it worked pretty well!

Our room that we used for our dining room had other problems, because of our sand floors. We had four metal chairs and a metal table, each with four legs. Now imagine yourself going to the beach and having a picnic and you brought four chairs and a table. You set the table and you have soup for supper. You sit on your chair, and the one leg sinks in the sand five inches, the other leg three inches, another leg two inches, and the fourth is left hanging in the air. Butch is sliding off his chair, Elaine is trying to hold on and eat soup at the same time, Sandy is crying, and I'm laughing my head off. (Who said it's no fun to be a missionary?)

I decided on Christmas day I would go see Mr. Verdis to see if he would sell me a few bags of cement. I never dreamed that Christmas would be celebrated in a fanatical Islamic city. Mr. Verdis was an Italian. He had deserted the Italian army several years earlier and escaped through the desert and ended up in Timbuktu. Somewhere along the way, he picked up a Tunisian woman who lived with him. He earned his living as a contractor working for the French administration in Timbuktu. Some of his landmarks were the "Palace of Justice" (courthouse), the Maternity, and the marketplace. These were all mud brick buildings faced with a soft white stone called *alhor*, which was mined in the desert. He lived in the main marketplace over the top of a store in an apartment that had been occupied by the C&MA missionaries prior to World War II.

It was now about 10:00 AM on Christmas Day, and he politely invited me in, and we sat down, and as was customary in this hot, dry climate, he offered me a drink. He said, "I can give you some cognac," and I responded that I didn't drink anything alcoholic, to which he immediately said, "Oh, then how about a beer?" To him beer was nonalcoholic and was considered a soft drink. I explained to him that I did not drink beer either. By now he was thinking I'm crazy. The poor man could not believe that I would be satisfied with water! He poured me a glass of water. I then began to explain to him that I was a missionary and had moved to Timbuktu with my wife and two young children. I was not telling him anything new, as Madame LeBoydeck had already shared this news all over town. This is known as *radio yobou* or market radio. He reminded me in a very kind way that today was Christmas, a holiday. That was a nice way of saying, "I do not have any cement today." The following day a couple of donkeys arrived with several bags of cement, and I had my first experience of trying to make concrete out of sand that was so fine that it seemed like the cement just ate it up and it "caked up" during the mixing process. I finally found that it required much more water than normally would be used, and contrary to what I was taught in trade school, adding more water in the mix did not weaken the cement or concrete. By sunset, I managed to get a cement floor down, troweling it into the evening with the light of an Aladdin lamp. This was progress; we now had a kitchen, bedroom, and dining room with cement floors.

It was several months later before we attempted to do anything with the living room floor. It remained a "sand box" where the children could play. The living room was dark, as there were no windows in it; the only light was if you opened the door. The door opened directly onto the street or alley and thus it could not be opened if you wanted any privacy or valued anything in the room. We had brought a wooden keg of nails with us that was about twelve inches in diameter. I hired Baba, a mason, and had him cut two holes in the sixty-centimeter (twenty-four-inch) mud wall about six and half feet off of the floor or road. Emptying out the keg, we used it as a form and built two port holes with alhor, one on each side the door. These were small enough to provide security, but allowed light into the room. Even today these two small round windows are a matter of curiosity to people passing by.

Eventually we cut a door in the kitchen that opened toward the market, which was located on a wide boulevard that made a ring around the old city and divided newer areas in town, which were laid out more or less in blocks. We put a screen door on this door to try to keep out the flies. We also cut a small window into the kitchen to let out some heat from the wood stove.

Just inside the door was a fifty-five-gallon drum for our water supply. We started by carrying buckets of water from the well to the house, but we soon hired a young man as our water boy. His name was Aldyumat, but everybody called him by his nickname Touridya. He was a Bella and lived in Bella Farandi, a section on the east side of town where Bellas lived who had been slaves to the Tuaregs. Therefore he spoke Tamasheq. Touridya worked for us and other missionaries when we were on furlough for the next twenty or more years. Besides working for us, he had millet and sorghum fields near the river that he and his wife cultivated during the rainy season.

How Did We Live?

Stories of its glorious past and the exotic-sounding name conjure up false images of this small, hot, sandy brown town. Visitors would ask not only *why* we were here, but *how* we would live here. Yes, daily life was different in Timbuktu. Routine tasks in America were never routine in Mali. For example, in meal preparation, if you wanted bread, you first had to sift your flour to attempt to get rid of most of the bugs and worms. Then you mixed your milk from powder. You would knead the dough and then let it rise, hoping the yeast was not too old, and then knead it again, and put it in the oven, which had caused the temperature in the already-hot house to increase even more.

Daily activities were not only time consuming, but Timbuktu life also required much planning. Food (especially fruits and grain) and freight could only be shipped north to Timbuktu during the high water season, so this required planning. With our kerosene lights and refrigerators and gasoline-powered washing machine, not to mention our motorcycle and eventual car, fuel was critical to us. Sometimes both food and fuel were ended up being rationed by the government to ensure that supplies would last until the next shipping season.

Water

We got our water from two sources. The closest source was just across the marketplace. It was open and about thirty feet deep. Of course, there were no pumps, so water was brought up manually. Metal buckets were not allowed, as they damaged the sides of the well, so the buckets dropped down into the well were made from goat skins, with some holding as much as five gallons of water. The rope that was used was also made from cowhide or goat skin that had been cut in strips about half an inch wide and then braided with three strands together, making it very strong. There were times when the well would go dry or the water table would recede. Not only did the water table recede, but the well also became a receptacle for the sand blowing in the air. It was then necessary to go down to the bottom and dig out the sand.

There was also a cone well—a deep hole dug in the ground but without any cement to hold the walls. The cone well, dug by slaves years ago, was about one hundred feet in diameter at the top and about twenty feet across the bottom or at the water level. Vegetable gardens were planted around the sides of it on terraces. People took water from the well to water their plants on the sides of the depression.

The water brought up from the cone well was green with algae. But we preferred this water to the water from the closer well, as that water would often have maggots in it. Sometimes pieces of the cowhide or goat skin rope would break off, fall into the well, rot, and get maggots or worms in it.

The ring for the barrel lid was very useful to us, as before filling the barrel with water, we put a piece of muslin sheet over the open end and clamped it with the metal clamp, which secured the sheet. Then the buckets or goat skins of water were poured over it, straining out the algae, worms, and maggots. After two buckets of water, the algae would have to be scrapped off of the muslin sheet.

Of course, using this muslin sheet did not purify the water. The water was used for cooking, bathing, and cleaning. For drinking water, we first boiled it for about five minutes over our wood stove (which also heated up the house even hotter). Then we poured it into another bucket that contained a stone filter. This filtered water was then poured into a clay water jug. This was a cooling process, as the jug would sweat and the dry air would evaporate it, causing the water to cool. Eventually we quit boiling the water, as the French told us that it made the water less healthy (for some reason), and like them, we merely used the stone filter. This saved on wood consumption and having to add more unwanted heat to our home. Stone filters had to be cleaned every day or so to remove the algae from them.

Most of the town got their water from these two water holes. Both wells were in constant use all day and into the night. These wells provided a business for many Bellas. The Bella men would fill their sheepskins with water by walking down into the water in their bare feet and standing knee deep in the water. Along with their sheep or goat skins, they carried a calabash or gourd in their hand, which was used as a dipper to fill the animal skin. When the skin was full, the neck was tied shut with a piece of leather rope, and then it was lifted onto the head. There were ten to twelve gallons of water in the skin. The Bellas were strong, especially their legs, as they walked up the side of the well with roughly 180 pounds of water on their heads. This was carried throughout the town as the Bella called out *"Hari koy, hari koy"* or water chief or water man. People would purchase the water for five francs a bag or about two cents. The skin was emptied into large, burned clay pots. Every household had several large clay vessels for holding water, which was used in cooking, bathing, and drinking.

Sometimes we'd buy goatskins of water from the Bella water carriers, but more often Touridya would roll a fifty-five-gallon drum to the well and fill it through the larger bung hole on the lid of the drum using an empty two-gallon motor oil can that had the bottom cut out as a funnel. After filling the drum, he would pull it over on its side and roll it through the loose sand to the house, which was a distance of about four hundred feet away. Four-year-old Butch was always at his side with his hands on the barrel helping him push the barrel. Then the water was transferred by bucket from the outside drum into the drum inside. That was our running water!

Water was also carried upstairs to the bathroom to another fifty-five-gallon drum that was used for bathing and flushing the toilet. The bathroom contained a basin, toilet, and shower. The shower was a unique French fabrication consisting of a large bucket with a sprinkling can head mounted on the bottom. Inside the bucket was a plunger type mechanism with a stopper on it, attached to a lever on the top of the bucket. The lever extended over the side of the bucket and either a small chain or a rope was attached to the lever. You would fill the bucket and lift it high over your head to a hook that was attached to a log that supported the roof. You needed to be ready for your shower, as often water was spilt over the rim of the bucket while you were lifting it over your head to the hook. Of course, Sandy and Butch had to take their showers along with one of us. Once a tourist used our shower, and Elaine heard her hollering from the shower, "Oh, if only my mother could see me now."

Masons also required large amounts of water for mixing mud for bricks, mortar, and plaster. The masons used a "daba" and their bare feet. The daba was a short-handled hoe used to break up the mud and to stir it, along with tramping it with the feet. A wooden mold was used to form the bricks, which were about eight inches wide, sixteen inches long, and four inches thick. The whole town is built of mud, but there is no mud or dirt in the town, since Timbuktu is built on two sand dunes.

During the rainy season, mud washed from the rooftops and the outside walls of the houses. After a hard rain, the mud would be carried away with the water as it rushed through the streets and alleyways going down to the lowest part of the town into a small lake, which happened to be just behind our house. During the dry season, the lake would almost disappear, thus exposing the mud that had accumulated during the rainy season after the water had evaporated. The mud was made again into bricks and used again in construction. When water in the lake covered the mud, the closest mud deposits were three miles out of town. This mud was transported in sacks made from grass mats and carried on the backs of donkeys.

Laundry

Regarding laundry, when we were in language school in Paris, we observed a demonstration in a department store where they were demonstrating a newly designed plunger for washing clothes. In 1951, France had very few washing machines, so clothes were put into a large, galvanized can about the size of a large trash can. This was filled with water, soap, and some blue cubes that looked like chalk, usually tied in a sock. After soaking for a while, a funnel-shaped plunger with a wooden handle was used to plunge up and down, causing the clothes to turn or gyrate. The new invention being demonstrated was that they added a spring in the bottom of the plunger so now you only had to push down and the spring would pop it back up! People excitedly watched this fascinating innovation! In fact, that's the way we washed our clothes in Algeria. In Timbuktu, we used a fifty-five-gallon drum with a plunger, but we were old fashioned and did not have a spring built into our plunger. Our laundry drum sat on bricks with a fire under it to heat the water.

The fifty-five-gallon drums sure came in handy for water and washing! The drums had been shipped from the States filled with items such as clothing, sheets, glassware, and pots and pans. There were no container ships in those days, so we packed our belongings in steel barrels, which had a lid held with a ring that clamped around the top. This could either be locked with a padlock or spot welded to keep thieves from breaking into it.

Energy Needs

Wood was very scarce and expensive in Timbuktu. Everybody cooked over wood fires or small charcoal burners fashioned by blacksmiths. During the rainy season, people from up the river, (south, as the river flowed north) where wooded areas still existed, could bring their boats into flooded areas miles away from the main river channel. There they harvested a very hard red wood. When the river was at its highest, a small hand-dug canal came from Koriome to Timbuktu, allowing small native-crafted boats to come all the way into town. This canal emptied into a pond just behind our house so the wood was brought almost to our door. We would buy boatloads of wood, and Touridya would cut it with an axe into lengths to fit our wood stove. We had a storage area at the back of the house that we would fill, as this wood was only available for less than a month before the water would recede again.

Part of every missionary's outfit was a Servel kerosene refrigerator. It had a five-gallon tank and burned an Aladdin lamp wick. This was our most prized possession. It made ice and kept food cold and refreshed us often. The kerosene's quality varied. High-quality kerosene would burn cleaner. Poor quality would encrust the wick and cause soot, making it necessary to trim the wick often. A yellow flame indicated that the wick was dirty or the kerosene was bad. It always amazed me that with a little fire you could make ice, if you had a blue flame. I was never quite sure how burning a wick under a refrigerator made it cold, but it did.

Communications

Communications were poor, as you'd expect being in a town that is synonymous with being at the end of earth. Until the French started the weekly flight to Goundam, 115 kilometers away, mail would come only sporadically by boat or across the desert. We were always anxious to get mail from home. My mother wrote every week, and our mail was delivered once a week on that weekly Saturday flight from Bamako. If the military had a truck going to Goundam, it would pick up the mail. If not, a postman on a camel would deliver the mail. If it came by truck, it would arrive at the post office on Saturday night. If it came by camel, then it would be Monday before we got our mail. Everybody gathered at the post office each Saturday night, and the mail was sorted by the light of kerosene lamps. Even as late as 9:00 PM, mail was put into our mailbox. For us, it was Boite Postale 3, and it has been since 1952.

As for mailing letters, it became very expensive if the envelope weighed more than five grams. Considering that there are 28 grams in an ounce, you can see this is a very light limit. We learned that a typed letter weighed less than one handwritten with ink. Sometimes they would weigh the letter and then put on the appropriate number of stamps, and then re-weigh the letter and find that it required even more stamps because of the weight of the first stamps!

After Independence came, the postal service deteriorated quickly. Initially there were no airplanes, and then one year after independence, Great Britain gave Mali three DC-3s. But these planes and subsequent ones were poorly maintained, and service was unreliable. Mali also had a shortage of pilots. I trained one Air Mali pilot to drive a car in Timbuktu. He had gone right from the donkey to the cockpit and never learned how to drive a car, even though he was flying commercial aircrafts for Air Mali.

We did not even have a radio for many years, so we had no idea what was going on in the outside world (and didn't really care), except for bits and pieces we would learn from the weekly mail that arrived when sandstorms allowed the plane to land at Goundam. Once while preaching in a small, remote village, I was astounded to come across a man living in a grass hut listening to a Zenith shortwave radio, but we didn't own one.

Fun and Games

Our entertainment consisted of things like waking up in the middle of night to the sound of two hundred growling camels behind our house.

Camel caravans would unload salt there. Camels roared like lions as the nomads tried to get them to lower themselves so that the slabs of salt could be unloaded. We also played board games and the children —like all children, they found fun and adventure everywhere playing with the African children in the sandy streets and sand dunes. They swam in the river, even though we discouraged it.

Our kids especially loved animals, and besides dogs and cats, we had a pet antelope, a lynx, and even a pet monkey named Booboo who was nothing but trouble. One time he stripped all the leaves from our flamboyant tree (trees are a precious resource in Timbuktu). Other times he would climb the tree and then cry incessantly as if he could not get down and needed help. He knew how to unlatch the windows and would constantly be going in and out and leaving them open so the ubiquitous swarms of flies would get into the house. Booboo would also pull the hair from the dog's tail. But the biggest problem was that he'd take one bite of any food he could get his hands on, knowing that then we wouldn't eat it and he'd get the rest of it. One day he found a basket of muffins and took one bite out of each muffin. That was just about the last straw! The lynx and house cats would play and sleep together. Unfortunately, our house cats would end up on somebody's dinner table, and our dogs would sometimes be poisoned. Poisoned meat was placed around town to kill packs of wild dogs that roamed the streets. Occasionally somebody would throw the poisoned meat over the wall into our compound to kill our pet dogs.

We had many good times with our small fifty cc motorcycle. With all four of us piled on, we would go down to the river on Saturday nights for picnics and a change in scenery. But even these excursions were problematic. In loose sand, the tire would get stuck, but the wheel would continue to turn, ripping the valve off the inner tube. Thorns causing flats were another constant problem—but it was just part of life there, and we knew to never leave home without a hand air pump. People thought, "Those crazy Americans!"

Sleeping, Eating, and Other Adventures

During the summer months, the heat was unbearable. Preceding every rain there was a dust storm with fierce winds. These storms were equivalent to the dust storms during the Dust Bowl years, with an approaching cloud of sand two miles high. It was impossible to keep sand out of your food. You soon learned when eating not to chew with your upper teeth touching your lower teeth unless you enjoyed grinding your teeth with sand. You would have to breathe through a handkerchief or towel to filter out the sand.

We slept outside to take advantage of cooler nights under the stars, but when a rainstorm hit in the middle of the night, it was a mad scramble to fold up our rollaway beds, get the nets down, and move everything inside before the drenching rain and wind would soak the bed with wet sand.

We ate well in this impoverished country. We would go to the meat market in the morning before the meat, hanging on hooks in the open-air market, had a chance to warm under the hot sun. When the meat would be weighed, I would tell the butcher to shoo the flies covering the meat because I did not want to pay for their weight too. We would eat a lot of lamb, some goat, and some beef, although beef was not always available. If a camel would get injured or die, camel meat would show up in the market. During the cold season, our garden and others produced tomatoes and eggplant. The eggplants became quite abundant, as boys would enter our garden and have fights, throwing the eggplants at each other. This served to spread the seeds all over the property.

Even something simple like getting a haircut was an adventure. Only one barber in town had clippers, because everybody else just had their heads shaved with razors. During an altercation, my barber cut somebody with his razor and ended up in prison, so I had to walk to prison and get my hair cut in the prison by this prisoner. The barbers were also the surgeons. They sharpened their knives on the soles of the feet—not shoes, but feet. The bottoms of their feet were like leather. If a person had a swollen leg or some such problem, the barber would make a cut to "bleed" the sore or infection. The barbers would also be the ones to make the scars on babies for tattoo like tribal markings. For example, the Songhai would cut three slits near the eyes to make three vertical lines of scars. They would rub in ashes to make it infected so that it would not heal but make a scar.

Medical Services

Like water, wood, communications, and other basic needs, medical services were very limited. Basically, only three or four treatments were available. If you had diarrhea or some other stomach ailment, you were given charcoal to eat. If you had an infection or skin ulcer, it would be wrapped in a "humid bandage" of permanganate solution or a sulfur paste. If you had congestion, about twenty little jars would be heated and then stuck on your chest with the vacuum formed from the heat. They would remain there with the heat drawing the blood to the surface. After they were removed, you looked like a waffle iron from the marks left by the jars.

The combination of the lack of medical facilities and uncertainty of travel caused concern. Dangers presented themselves daily. On one occasion, after our youngest daughter Diane was born, we watched from the rooftop Touridya rolling a fifty-five-gallon drum over to the well to get water. Sandy and Diane were following along. Sandy was three years old, and Diane two. They had to pass by the little market where the nomads would bring their animals to sell to the butchers. People were sitting under a few trees that provided shade. Others had put up grass mats for shade and were sitting under them. As Touridya was rolling the barrel full of water back to our kitchen door, a ram came running full speed behind them with his head down and hit Sandy from behind, and while she was getting up, it knocked Diane down. We felt helpless as this happened repeatedly as we watched from the rooftop. Touridya chased the ram away, but the people in the market began to laugh and clap their hands. For them it was very amusing, but for us it was horrifying.

One morning we found a dead scorpion in Diane's diaper. I guess urine can kill a scorpion, as the scorpion never stung her. If something bad would have happened to our children, traveling for treatment would have been challenging. After the difficult, long drive to Goundam, we never knew if the plane would land at Goundam to pick us up because of sandstorms and too much dust in the air. A person might have to wait several days for one, and there were no accommodations there. One time a missionary couple came to spend a week with us. They left to catch the flight in Goundam, and after the arduous three-hour drive, they learned that the weekly flight could not land because of a sandstorm. With no flight for another week, they had to turn around and ride back to Timbuktu. The woman was pregnant and tragically lost the baby on this rough round trip across the desert. Not knowing for sure if you could travel and then the hazards of travel were always something that we had to trust God for and try not to be stressed or worried about, but it was always in the back of your mind, and contingencies had to be planned. When Air Mali was eventually formed, it soon earned the nickname, "Air Maybe." Since so many things would go wrong with plans, tourists invented a saying to explain the constant delays and disappointments, "WAWA," which stands for West Africa Wins Again. This dismissive statement said with a shrug seemed to lighten the spirits of frustrated or angry people.

The biggest difficulty during these early years was a feeling of isolation in this remote outpost of Timbuktu. The closest missionaries to us where four hundred kilometers away in Gao. After we moved to Timbuktu, Elaine did not see another Christian woman for the entire first term, except for a brief visit from my sister-in-law and brother over Christmas one year and a brief visit with Ann Zimmerman in Gao. She experienced loneliness, not having fellowship with other Christian women. An anti-American mood prevented us from becoming close to the French couples in Timbuktu. The Communist influence was strong after independence in Mali as well. This presented challenges to us when trying to befriend others.

Chapter 7.

Establishing Our Ministry

"God uses men who are weak and feeble enough to lean on him." J. Hudson Taylor

We felt we needed to have a meeting place, and we also desired to have a Christian bookstore, so we divided the storage room with a mud wall. One side served as a classroom and the other a store. There were already two doorways that opened onto the marketplace. These had been bricked up with mud bricks, but the lintels were still in place. I had a carpenter make up door frames and doors that I would cover with some aluminum corrugated roofing pans. They were shiny and stood out, being the only doors like it in town. Inside we whitewashed the walls, put down a cement floor, and made bookshelves out of rough boards, and in the bookstore, we put on the wall in large letters 1 Timothy 2:5.

THERE IS ONE GOD AND ONE MEDIATOR BETWEEN GOD AND MAN, THE MAN, CHRIST JESUS.

Our mission in Niger had a Christian bookstore in Niamey, so we ordered our supplies through them. The supplies would come over the road from Niamey to Gao and from there by riverboat, Dan Zimmerman being our liaison person for shipping in Gao. It was necessary to have our supplies in Gao before the riverboats would stop running from mid-February to the middle of August.

It is virtually impossible to have a Christian bookstore in a city that is 99 percent Muslim, unless you have some bait to attract clients. We were fishing for men. The bait would be selling schoolbooks and supplies. Not only was it bait to attract people, but it also *allowed* men and women to be seen coming into our store. If we only had Christian materials, anybody entering our store would face a backlash and persecution. This way they could say they had only entered for school supplies.

At that time, there were two schools in Timbuktu. There was also a Nomadic school at Koriome. Most children did not have any books. In the classroom, several students shared the same book, or the teacher would copy from a book onto the blackboard. Many parents were anxious for their children to have their own books. In the elementary school, they used a curriculum from first grade through eighth grade called Mamadou et Binetta. There were no stores in Timbuktu selling school books or supplies, so we handled books, dictionaries, notebooks, and other supplies. Ballpoint pens were not allowed, as the children were required to write with a straight pen, and each letter had to be formed as calligraphy with certain parts of a letter broad and other parts narrow. All the writing was script, and students never printed.

Paper was also scarce, but each child received a chalkboard that was about nine by twelve inches, and they had a chalk pencil (very hard piece of calcium about an eighth of an inch in diameter that was sometimes held in a metal stick). Looking at a wood pencil, the calcium would be the equivalent to the lead, and the wood would be the equivalent to the metal tube that held the chalk. With a damp cloth, the chalkboard could be wiped clean and used forever. So this was our bait to bring people into the store, and it was successful and very much appreciated. With every sale, the customer received a gospel tract in either French or Arabic. We had a variety of booklets that we obtained from the Scripture Gift Mission in London. They were colorful and printed in many languages. Our French Bibles were obtained from La Maison de la Bible or Bible House in Paris, the Arabic Bibles came from Beirut, Lebanon. Most school books and supplies came from publishers in France. There was a small mark-up on the school supplies to help offset the cost of Christian literature. Literally thousands of pieces of literature were distributed through the bookstore.

The other room next to the bookstore was our classroom where we conducted evangelistic children's meetings several afternoons each week. We taught scripture memorization, songs, and flannel-graph lessons. The attendance was very irregular, ranging from one or two to as many as twenty children, as the adults were still afraid to be seen entering the chapel. Both the door to the classroom and the bookstore opened to the marketplace, so anybody coming in could be seen.

Butch was the attraction, as he was the only white kid in town, and he had picked up the language quickly. He usually had some toy that fascinated the kids, which was like a magnet in drawing children. Sometimes our meetings were interrupted when a parent or two would storm into the classroom and snatch their children and begin to beat them unmercifully out in the road because they were listening to the *Toubob* or Christian. The beatings were severe, and sometimes it would take several weeks before we would see them again. We felt terrible and totally helpless when children would be beaten for attending our meetings. One of these boys named Alisane became good friends with Butch, and I still see him whenever I am back in Timbuktu.

One afternoon while at the bookstore, I was visited by the *Cadi* or the Muslim judge. This man was actually empowered by the French government as the judge to judge many of the trials that would not conflict with French law and especially religious Islamic law. He was fluent in French, Arabic, Moor, and Songhai. He read the verse of Scripture on the wall and then said to me sarcastically, "That's not true." I probably should have answered a little more discreetly, but as a young man of twenty-five, I said, "It is true, and anybody who says different is a liar because that is the word of God." He immediately interpreted my statement as calling Mohammed a liar and stormed out into the market, shouting to everyone that I called Mohammed a liar and infuriated the people to the point of causing a riot. A crowd gathered, yelling and chanting. I had time to close the door and lock it, and I fled out through the storage area into the house. We kept the store closed for a few days until things had settled down. Generally the Songhai people are very calm and friendly. Fortunately, Cadi was not well-liked in town, and so his influence waned. The local French commandant may have also played a role in calming the community without our knowledge.

We had not yet begun to hold regular Sunday services because I needed permission from the French government. This had to come from the minister of interior in the capital of Bamako and pass through the channels of government bureaucracy. I wrote a letter under the cover of the commandant du circle (the local commander). I never received a response. After waiting a couple months, Madame LeBoydek told me that the adjutant to the commandant was a communist and that my letter stopped in his office. She suggested that I go "over his head."

So I did and made a trip of one thousand kilometers to Bamako. Now my French was very limited in both my understanding as well as my speaking. I learned that the higher positions in government were up at Kouliba, a small mountain town just outside of the city. I took a taxi and went to the office, where I met the secretary of the gentleman I wanted to see. I was asked if I had an appointment, and my answer was no, but that I had come all the way from Timbuktu to see him. The secretary then explained to me that the minister was, *"Occupe au cabinet."* My understanding and interpretation of this was that he had gone to the toilet, when in fact he was in a cabinet meeting. Cabinet in French is a toilet room. So I patiently waited on the veranda.

After an hour, I began to wonder how long it took for a Frenchman to go to the toilet. I had explained to the secretary why I was there and gave him a copy of the letter that I had addressed to him months before. These official letters are always dated by the recipient and signed for when delivered. Apparently the secretary did some research and discovered the letter had never been received in their office. My patience paid off, as just before noon, I was invited into the office and met the gentlemen. We only spent a couple minutes together, and he obviously had been briefed by his secretary. He simply said that I could return to Timbuktu and begin holding church services. I asked if I needed written permission, and his answer was, "The commandant will be advised before you have time to arrive back in Timbuktu."

We wanted to hold our services in our living room by converting it into a chapel. But with the sand floors, there was no way to set up chairs, because their legs would just sink into the sand. Upon arriving back home, I purchased about twenty-five donkey loads of mud, which I mixed with sand and water to "cement" the floor with about three inches of mud. It took about a couple of weeks for it to dry, since there was no way for the sun to dry it and the humidity was high inside the house. While the living room was about sixteen feet by sixteen feet there was a large pillar about two feet by three feet right in the center of the room. But with our small congregation, we would be able to work around the pillar problem.

The entire population was practicing Muslims. As we walked through town, the women would greet us with *"Dyahenem Idye,"* meaning "child of hell" or "child of the pit." We assumed it was just a friendly greeting, and we would reply *"nda lafia"* (with peace). But what we thought was a friendly greeting was in fact a curse. We soon learned that traditional greetings were long and drawn out when you not only asked how a person was but you would also ask about the entire family, mother, father, children, and any other family living in the town, and even their animals. This could take five minutes, as it was often repeated more than once. I would sit with the old men in the market and try to pick up the language. They would make fun of me but allowed me to join them.

Language learning was slow, but we were fortunate to have a small dictionary and grammar book that had been prepared by Pere Yacouba. Pere Yacouba was a Catholic priest who came to Timbuktu at the beginning of the twentieth century. He learned the language well and the traditions of the people. He soon married a Songhai woman and had a sizeable family. Of course, he was no longer considered a "white father," but was employed by the French government as a liaison officer between the military and the local population.

Timbuktu had only been conquered a couple years prior to this, about 1896, and there were still several ambushes into the 1920s by Tuareg tribesman wiping out platoons who were on maneuvers in the desert. The French had a military base along the Niger River, one on the south side of Timbuktu called Fort Bonnier, and another on the northeast corner of Timbuktu next to the old Sankore mosque.

There is no record of Yacouba ever having any converts other than his male children, who turned out to be nominal Catholics. Coincidently, the house we rented in Gao belonged to Jean Marou, who was Yacouba's son-in-law. Yacouba was buried in the "Christian" cemetery, but his grave is in a unique position with his head on the north and feet in the south. The Muslims bury their dead in this position with the body on its side facing Mecca to the east. All the other graves in the Christian or European cemetery have the head and feet buried east and west. Yacouba's wife was still living when we arrived in Timbuktu. She always remained a Muslim. She did keep a room upstairs in their mud house as a museum to his memory. I especially recall seeing his very old, primitive typewriter.

By now, we had a few African Christian soldiers who attended our Sunday morning services. The military men were from Guinea, Ivory Coast, Dahomey, Togo, Upper Volta, and the southern part of the French Sudan. French colonies received their independence in 1960. These former colonies changed their names. Upper Volta became Burkina Faso, Ivory Coast strictly used its French name, Cote d'Ivoire, Dahomey became Benin, and the French Sudan became Mali. All of these soldiers were part of the French army prior to independence and were intermixed with the French soldiers. Because of the pillar, we set the chairs on one side of the room, and seldom did we have more than six to eight in attendance. This depended on whether or not the soldiers had duty. There were no other

Christians in town. Occasionally the military members of our congregation would be sent deep into the desert to maintain peace with the Tuaregs.

During this first term, Touridya made a profession of faith. I never knew how sincere he was, as he would later be seen doing his Muslim prayers, but he continued to be our dear friend and helper. Toward the end of our first term, a typical congregation would include Lamin, Touridya (who was never paid to come to church, but may have thought it helped his job security), and random kids from town.

Bebe was an old deaf and dumb man. During the early years in Timbuktu, I could communicate better with him than anyone else since I couldn't speak the language either. We communicated with gestures. He was my first student. This short, old former mason would come every evening, and I would give Bible lessons. I started with creation and eventually got to the crucifixion. Maybe the best thing that ever happened to me while in Timbuktu happened when I was returning from our garden and I saw Bebe communicating with a small group of men along the street and Bebe had drawn the three crosses in the sand. Although he could not speak, he was communicating the gospel to other men.

Seeking Relief in Dakar

The months of April, May, and June were extremely hot months, with the outside temperatures in the sun going as high as 140 degrees and shade temperatures to 107. Temperatures during the day in the house were as high as 104. At the same time, the humidity was extremely low, which made the heat a little more bearable, but at the same time, very dangerous because of dehydration. The French had banned their military from having children under the age of two living in Timbuktu because children under two often died from dehydration. We had been excused from this rule, but on the advice of the military doctor, he suggested Elaine go out to Dakar on the west coast with Sandy during these months of extreme heat. These were some hard decisions, as it would be expensive for the airfare to fly from Goundam to Dakar via Bamako. We were able to arrange for her to stay in a room in Dakar at the Protestant "Foyer" or guest house that was operated by the French Reformed Church. The Lord graciously supplied sufficient funds for her airline ticket, along with Sandy's which was 10 percent of an adult fare. The French army gave her a ride in a vehicle from Timbuktu to the airstrip in Goundam.

The sun beat down on the aluminum plane, turning it into an oven. There was no air conditioning and no air circulation until the plane got up to the cruising altitude of ten thousand feet. Looking out the window, northern Mali looks like dry, cracked leather, crisscrossed with livestock paths radiating from water holes and wells. Scattered clusters of huts and single trees freckle the landscape. The land looks ill—frail and scarred, like the faces of the people struggling to survive on it. Looking down on the towns, the maze of narrow, crooked streets, and the simple, uneven, rectangular buildings make the city look like something drawn by an ambitious child with a new Etch-a-Sketch. Sprinkled around the outskirts of town are clusters of dome-shaped huts made out of woven grass—the homes of the Tuaregs. Their makeshift corrals consisting of fences made of branches taken from thorn bushes form black outlines of polygons against the yellow earth.

It was so bumpy, it felt like the wings had fallen off. Just as the plane reached cruising altitude, it began to descend to the next stop in Mopti. While airline staff refueled the plane, a small breakfast was served in the airport bar courtesy of the airline. It consisted of coffee and bread and butter. Sometimes the butter had a rancid taste, but passengers enjoyed it, especially since many had left their last meal in the lined paper bag on the back of the airplane seat in front them. By the time the plane was refueled and the paperwork completed, the plane was again suffocatingly hot. Besides the full complement of passengers on board, live chickens were always part of the hand baggage carried on by passengers. There was audio entertainment on these flights, just roosters crowing. It also was not unusual to have live sheep on board with their legs tied together. Years later, they would be slipped into burlap bags with just their heads sticking out with the burlap tied around their necks. The burlap served as diapers and made the plane easier to clean—that's progress! Typically sheep were shipped near a feast day to families living in the capital, as they were much cheaper to purchase in the northern Mali. So sometimes it was not only the roosters singing but often a duet, trio, or choir with its baa, baa and cock-a-doodle-doo. It was amusing to us but normal in West Africa.

In Bamako, Elaine and Sandy boarded another Air France aircraft, this one a larger DC4 that had some air conditioning, and after two-plus hours, they landed in Dakar, where as a sailor I had spent five days back in 1946. This was a much larger airport, built by the U.S. army during World War II. It served flights from Europe going to South America (Receife, Brazil, and Dakar were the two shortest points between South America and Africa) and even a Pan Am flight from the U.S. Dakar was the capital of French West Africa, and the only American representative in all of French West Africa was a consul here who was responsible to the American Embassy in Paris.

Elaine and Sandy arrived at the Foyer. The Foyer was located near a restaurant where you could eat in or order their *"Plat du Jour"* and take it out. A convenient set of pans that stack with a carrier was common, as many people bought their meals this way. Sandy, being just a year old, was barely walking, but somehow Elaine managed to get to the restaurant, acquire the meal, and take it back to her room to eat.

Meanwhile, back in Timbuktu, I, as chief cook and bottle washer, was learning to "batch it" with Butch, but not very well. I had developed an infection in my knee, which went from bad to worse. It was very painful, and to top it all off I had to walk nearly a mile to the dispensary every day to have it cleaned, soaked, and dressed and then walk home. Probably the hardest thing to endure was the kids on the road as they would see me limping in pain were laughing and calling "Toubabu, Toubabu" and mocking me. This was somewhat normal in this part of Africa, as there was no sympathy for those who were suffering.

Eventually the doctor cut three holes in my knee to drain it. The holes were all interconnected. Warm compresses of potassium permanganate were attached to the knee and left to soak for about thirty minutes. Then a piece of gauze about a yard long and an inch wide was stuffed into one of the holes and out of another one of the holes and then drawn through from one end to the other to clean out the wound. The same procedure was done for the remaining hole. Some pomade containing penicillin was then inserted into the wound and a dressing put on and then my walk back home. I put up with this for a couple of weeks with what seemed to be little improvement. I decided to see if I could scrape up some money and join Elaine in Dakar. After being on my own for over a month and being a big baby with pitying myself, Butch and I made a trip to Dakar. We took the kids to the beach, which they enjoyed. In the water there were a lot of jelly fish, and the last thing I wanted was to get stung, so we found a nice swimming pool along the beach where they pumped in sea water to the pool. We enjoyed cooling off in this pool. My knee was still oozing with infection, but after a couple of trips to the pool, the saltwater completely healed my sores, even though I will carry the three scars on my knee to my grave. Not only was my infection healed, but Elaine had gotten a large "oriental" sore on her leg that failed to heal for months, and the Lord used His saltwater to heal her also.

By July we decided to return to Timbuktu. The rainy season had just started. While we were away, there had been a large rain. Some termites had worked their way up the wall and through the roof, which was mud. The rain found the hole and began to flush down the hole into our bedroom onto the bookshelf that hung on the wall. What a mess! The first order of business was to get a couple buckets of dirt and get up on the top roof and attempt to plug the hole, which had grown from a little termite hole to a hole that I could put my fist through. The patch job didn't take too long, but the clean-up in the bedroom was something else. All of our books had gotten wet with mud, plus we found that the termites are also "bookworms" and apparently read through every page, leaving small, pin-size holes from cover to cover. They also ate all the jackets off of our tapes; however they didn't seem to like the tape itself. Someone needs to develop paper that is termite proof! We learned that after the first good rain every year, we'd have to go up and plug all of the termite holes in the mud roof. Otherwise the rain would come right down into the house.

A Special Christmas

A couple days after our first anniversary in Timbuktu the Lord blessed us with another daughter, Diane Elaine. She was the first American girl to be born in Timbuktu and possibly the first white girl to be born there, as the French returned to France to have their children. It was early on Christmas Eve that Elaine decided we needed to go to the mud-walled maternity. It was the coldest night on record during our twenty years in Timbuktu. It was 40 degrees or 4 Celsius. It is still known as "the year of the cold." The building had no electricity or running water, just three rooms in a row with a veranda on the south side. The bed had metal slats that looked like leaf-springs off of a truck. There was a mattress made out of burlap and stuffed with straw. I alerted Dr. Pincon that Elaine was in labor. He was at his home, which was between the fort and the prison. He was a military doctor but served the local population as well. The French doctors had very little experience in obstetrics, as that was handled by midwives. The midwife in Timbuktu had a lot of experience but absolutely no formal training.

At home we were getting together what we would need to take with us to the maternity: wash cloth, towel, soap, filtered drinking water, a basin, bed sheets, pillow, a blanket, some toilet paper, diapers, and even our own kerosene lamp. None of this was provided to families. Dr. Pincon was kind and came with a military truck. I had the little motorcycle, but that was hardly the appropriate transportation for taking a lady about to deliver a baby. We got set up at the maternity with the dim light of the lantern and a flash light. The door on the room was made of the same metal as the shutters, with slots to let the air through. The wind was blowing fiercely in the windows across the delivery table and out the door. Elaine was freezing. The midwife was there, and Dr. Pincon said he was going out but would be back later. Of course it was Christmas Eve, and all the French were having a big party, which would be interrupted by midnight mass. There was never a resident Catholic priest in Timbuktu, but there were a couple priests up the river in Dire about 90 kilometers away by boat and they would come over to celebrate mass.

Midnight came, and about 12:30 Diane appeared. I'll never forget the sight as the midwife took Diane by her feet and dumped her into a basin of ice cold water. There was no need to spank her to see if she was breathing. The minute she hit the water and the wind blew over her, she gasped for breath and cried. She wiped her off with our towel and handed her to me to put on a diaper and shirt. The midwife knew nothing about diapers or shirts. African babies never wore diapers, and many never wore underwear until they turned three or four years old or even older. Diane was then wrapped in a blanket, and hopefully would survive the cold air. Elaine was still shivering when Dr. Pincon arrived sometime after 1:00 AM. He was advised by the midwife that everything went well. He put his cold stethoscope on her and checked her pulse, looked at Diane, and said, *"Bonne nuit."* About 5:00 AM, we could hear the imam calling out to the faithful to prayer. It was also a reminder to us to thank God for the safe arrival of Diane and also the safe arrival of Jesus nearly two thousand years before as Mary lay in the straw clutching God's gift to the world on a cold, wintry night.

That afternoon, George Saouma, a Lebanese merchant who had recently purchased an old Citroen car, took us home. We had put up a Christmas tree and had placed gifts under it. The tree was made up of thorn branches tied together. We placed Diane under the tree, along with Butch and her sister, Sandy. The tree was on the upstairs veranda, and in the marketplace below there were the cattle, sheep, goats, donkeys, and camels. All seemed to be welcoming Diane to her new home. This would comprise our family. Butch was now four and half years old, holding his new sister in his arms, Sandy, now a year and a half, looked on, while Mom and Dad took pictures. What a wonderful Christmas!

We paid the Songhai midwife with a leg of lamb. This mimicked the local customs at childbirth. The local people would not name their baby until after the seventh or eighth day. Waiting a week or even longer to name a baby is common among many ethnic groups in West Africa. People believe that this tradition developed because infant mortality was so high during childbirth and the first few days after birth, that by not naming the baby immediately made the loss of the child less personal and therefore less emotionally devastating. When the baby survived the first week or so, the family would host a big celebration and name the baby. At the baby-naming feast, a sheep would be slaughtered, and the midwife would be given a leg of lamb. The other three legs would be given to friends or people that they respected. Often we missionaries were fortunate enough to receive one of these legs of lamb.

I found that missionaries were sometimes very hard on converts when they sacrificed animals for such celebrations. Some missionaries thought that the converts were slipping back into Islam or their animistic religions. Although these practices may have started as a religious practice, they were clearly now merely a cultural event, not unlike the way we "slaughter" a turkey on Thanksgiving or celebrate Christmas traditions.

Over the next couple of months, the weather was kind to us, with cool almost-cold nights, but by noon time it was completely warm. In the early morning hours you would see people lined up along the east wall of the mud houses where the eastern sun was warming up the wall, much like the way we hugged the radiators as kids when we came into the house after playing in the snow. Most people shivered all night with no blanket. Nobody went to the market before about 9:30 in the morning, and the whole town seemed to be in slow motion. Our house was two stories in the front and one story in the back section. The rooftop of the back section was the play yard for the kids. It had a parapet wall about four and a half feet tall around it. Butch had a red wagon, and Sandy had a blue and white walker. They enjoyed playing on the roof top. By the end of March, it began to get hot. Our beds were "rollaway," which folded up and could be rolled on the casters out on to the roof, where we slept from April to mid-November. Once our mud houses warmed up, they stayed hot and didn't cool down, as the thick walls and roof held the heat. We strung a clothesline up to both hang the wash by day and at night we hung our mosquito nets on them. Wash was a daily chore, as there were no disposable diapers in those days, and even if there were, there would not have been a market for them, as the Africans did not "dipe" their kids.

By the time Diane was three months old, we often carried her in our arms as we walked on the roof. She would invariably reach and grab hold of the clothes line and would not let go. (The Africans told us that babies have enough strength in their hands that they can squeeze a snake to death. We never tried that!) As she was hanging on for dear life, I left her go and she just hung there while I went to get the camera. As a precaution, the bed was under her. I took a picture of this a unique way to dry diapers—just hang the kid out to dry.

River Ministry

During our first term, we started a vehicle fund to have some transportation. After moving to Timbuktu from Gao, we realized that at the rate funds were coming in, maybe we needed to reassess this need. There were no roads to go anywhere, just desert tracks that could be there one day and gone the next. "The wind bloweth where it listeth." (John 3:8). You have it but don't know where it came from or where it went. Other than some nomads in the desert who constantly were moving looking for food for their cattle, the greater population lived along the river, where they had water to drink, cook, and bathe and fish to eat. If they traveled, it was in small canoes made of pieces of wood that had been hewn from scrub trees and then holes burned into the pieces of wood that are sewed together to provide a boat to get out in the river to cast their nets or to cross to the other side.

We realized that while there was no highway, God had provided a vast waterway to reach the villages that dotted the shores of the Niger River. We had enough in our transportation fund to purchase a small fifteen-foot boat with a motor, but we had one obstacle, our general director, Rev. Joseph McCaba. Joe was opposed because of his experience of living in Niger along the river and he had witnessed how storms come up without notice, not necessarily rain storms but angry wind storms that could capsize a boat in a moment, to say nothing about the abundant crocodiles and hippos, which had their protective habitats. Somehow we prevailed. Soon we were ordering a boat from the Starcraft Boat Company in Goshen, Indiana, and a twenty-five-horsepower outboard motor from Montgomery Ward.

Both were shipped to Bridgeport Baptist Church, and my father-in-law, George Beswick, got two-by-fours and plywood and built a large case and packed it, including a lot of five-gallon jerry cans, life preservers, etc., and it was shipped to Africa. Within about two months it arrived on a barge at Koriome. Elaine and I unpacked it on the deck of the barge and slipped it into the canal. The crate would later provide wood to build kitchen cabinets, which as of 2006 were still being used. My father-in-law had fabricated a metal frame fastened to the gauntlets of the boat to support a canvas tarp that provided us shade from the sun. The frame was made from half-inch galvanized water pipe.

During the remainder of the last couple years of our first term, we put in hundreds of miles traveling to many villages where I preached and presented the gospel to village people, gave out simple medications such as aspirin, and treated several people, especially children, for burns. It was not unusual to find small children who had fallen into the open fires where mothers were cooking.

My first long trip was to the town of Gourma Rharous. We had heard in 1935 a man named Mohamed Lamin had been saved through the ministry of Mr. Bowman, a missionary with the Christian and Missionary Alliance. The Bowmans and other C&MA missionaries left Timbuktu and Gao around 1940 because of the war. It was now 1953, and Mohamed Lamin had not had any contact with a Christian for thirteen years. I had learned he was working as a *surveillante* (overseer) at a nomadic school. The French government required a certain number of nomadic children to go to school. The children received a dark blue "boubou" or gown, a grass mat shelter, and meals. They had been taken away from their parents, but some parents resisted, and often in the middle of the night the children were awakened and put on the back of a camel and taken back to the nomadic camp. When children would disappear, it was Mohammed Lamin's responsibility to locate them and bring them back to school.

My Songhai language was not the best, and neither was his, as his language was Tamasheq. I did not know if he had openly shared with others that he was a Christian, and I did not want to jeopardize his safety or his job. I knew it could cost him his job or even his life if it were known. The school was located very high up on the top of a sand dune overlooking the river, so we went down to my boat and went out in the middle of the river. There I tried my best to communicate the word of God. I did have a copy of the New Testament in Songhai, and I read to him. I began singing the few songs that I had learned in Songhai and even one that I learned in Tamasheq. Lamin just beamed! He joined in the singing, and together we sang songs that he had remembered. It was worth the hundred-mile one-way trip!

I spent the next day with him, having spent the night in a very primitive *campement.* My concern was that as the only Christian in the whole area, Lamin (we began to call him Lamin rather than his full name) needed to be discipled and have fellowship, but how could I shepherd him? During the night, while trying to sleep on a grass mat, the Lord caused me to think about bringing him back to Timbuktu. Lamin was basically a shepherd, and I asked him about shepherding. He explained that sheep reproduce once a year, but goats reproduce twice a year. I made a bargain with him, and that was that I would buy a hundred goats and he would shepherd them, and his pay would be that he would get all the milk from the goats. On top of that, the agreement would be that every other kid that would be born in the flock would belong to him. Thus he would be able to build his own flock. He was excited about the arrangement.

Within a month, I sent him enough money to buy a boat ticket from Gourma Rharous to Koriome for himself and his wife, Fatimata. When a nomad moves, he does not need a U-haul, but everything he owns fits on the back of a donkey. It's all wrapped up in a grass mat that is their bed plus a tea pot, as they can pretty much survive on tea with sugar Just behind our rented mud house was the "new market," where sheep, goats, cows, and camels were bought and sold. The butchers also came here to purchase animals that would be butchered and sold in the meat market the following day. It only took a few days to acquire one hundred goats and to turn over the flock to Lamin upon his arrival in Timbuktu. The Lord provided enough funds to purchase the hundred goats, most of which were she goats. This gave Lamin a flock to shepherd and provided my flock with a shepherd. Was I ever naïve! Here I was a Christian who was taught for years and had learned to trust people and assumed that because Lamin had been a Christian for fifteen years, he would have the same values as me. After all, he had been a Christian as long as I had been a Christian. Was I ever wrong!

Lamin was illiterate, spent at least thirteen years without seeing a Christian, and had gone thirteen years without hearing God's word. His wife was not a Christian. They had no children, owned only what was on their backs, and as soon as they had a way of earning a living, they discovered they had relatives they had never met before but who culturally they were responsible to feed. I began to hear, "Pastor, one of your goats died," and another time, "Pastor, a dog killed one of your goats." I never heard him say that one of his goats died. It was always one of mine. Instead of the flock growing, it was slowly diminishing. But here was a fifteen-year-old "baby" living in a culture that was anti-Christian and fanatically religious where they believe no one is responsible for his sin since God created us, and thus sin is not our problem but God's. God gets credit for both good and evil. The challenge of nurturing Lamin was great, but he did grow in his Christian faith, and in spite of being mocked by many, he stood faithful. Many years later, Fatimata, his wife, became a Christian, and I baptized her, along with Sandy, in the Niger River.

At first he put up a grass mat shelter northwest of our house about a kilometer away. Later, when the weather got cooler, we moved him to the southeast corner of town where the C&MA had a small piece of land that they had received a government *permit d'occuper*. They had dug a well on this land that was about fifty-five feet deep, and there was water in it. We decided to fence in the land that was thirty by forty meters. There was also a small mud building adjacent to the well that was four by six meters. To fence this in we used, fifty-five-gallon gasoline drums, to which I fastened a two-by-four on the side of each after having cut the top out of the drum. The drums were then spaced about ten feet apart and filled with sand. Barbed wire was then nailed to the two-by-fours. This is where we would plant a vegetable garden in the sand. Gasoline and kerosene fifty-five-gallon drums were plentiful because it was too costly to return the empty drums to the coast.

I learned a lesson after having put a nice fence around the property that was meant to protect it from animals and people. I should have remembered the Scriptures and the song, "The wise man built his house upon the rock," and not the sand. The barrels were sitting on the sand, and as the wind blew, it eroded the sand from beneath the drums, and within about a month they had all fallen over, and the barbed wire lay on the ground.

At any rate, by moving Lamin to the property, it would provide some security for our garden—at least we thought that it would. We learned that the desert will blossom if it is watered. During our cool season, we were able to grow peas, beans, corn, melons, lettuce, beets, cabbage, etc. Flowers would also grow. There was a season to plant in the beginning of November, then a season to water, weed, and then harvest. Another lesson we learned was the importance of properly preparing the soil. Commercial fertilizer was not available and was not needed the first year, as there were enough dehydrated nutrients in the ground. Subsequent years we sent for some manure. This was dug out of a corral where goats were kept at night. It looked great as the sacs were unloaded from the backs of donkeys, but the end result was horrific. The goats feed on thorns, and thus as they pass through, the goats became like a mechanical grain planter, and we ended up with beautiful beds of thorn bushes. It was a little bit like a computer; we learned what you put in is what you get out. This served as a warning regarding what we feed ourselves and others and reminded us of I Peter 1:23: *"Being born again, not of corruptible seed, but of incorruptible by the Word of God which liveth and abideth for ever."*

Our boat not only expanded our ministry but also provided many exciting trips for the children. We would see hippos resting in the reeds and crocodiles sunning themselves on the sandy banks. Hundreds of birds would flush from the water and riverbanks, particularly in winter when ducks and other waterfowl would migrate down from Europe to spend the winter along the Niger River. I would occasionally take the boat on duck-hunting trips with a Muslim friend. He wore thick, coke-bottle glasses but was a great shot and made sure we had duck for our table. We also would hunt wild warthogs on islands in the river. Because Muslims don't eat pork, this is one of the few wildlife species that has not been wiped out by overhunting. However, in recent years, many less-devout Muslims have acquired the taste for fresh pork and hunt warthogs frequently.

Once we took a trip in our boat to visit Frank and Eleanor in Gao, downriver four hundred kilometers away. For our return, we had planned to put our boat on the riverboat and ship it as freight back to Koriome and we would go as passengers. However, the employees of the boat company went on strike, so our only option was to launch out again in our boat going upstream against the wind and the current. It was the cool season, and the winds were coming from the north, bringing white caps. The children were still very small. Diane was barely one year old. We left early in the morning from Gao and got about 150 kilometers when we decided to stop for the day, and we pulled onto an island where a couple of families had a shelter and a fire going. We stayed in the boat with the kids lying on the bottom between the benches. The next day we set out again, and the wind was strong and the waves were splashing over the bow of the boat with the wind driving like a fierce rainstorm blowing in our faces as we all shivered. We finally made it to the other side, where the banks of the river provided some shelter, and after about two hours, we arrived at Gourma Rharous, where we stayed overnight and dried out in the *campement* and warmed up. We left early the next morning and arrived at Koriome about noon. There we sat in the shade of a tree until a truck would arrive and we could bargain with the driver to take our family, the motor, and gas cans to our house. By three in the afternoon, we were finally home exhausted and reflecting how foolish we were to make that eight hundred-kilometers trip as a family of five in my little fifteen-foot outboard motor boat. We had to carry all of our gas to get us to Gao and then purchase enough for our return trip, which would be all upstream and against the wind. Oh well, God was good to us and protected us even though it was foolish on our part to risk such a strenuous trip.

We had other close calls on the river. One time I volunteered to ferry my brother's boat down to Niamey. For Sandy's and my nephew Bob's Senior trip, we decided to take them, along with Diane and Bob's sister Bonnie, on a boat trip to Niamey, Niger. His boat was an eighteen-foot boat with a sixty HP Mercury outboard. My brother Frank and his wife followed as close to the river as possible, carrying extra fuel for us. From time to time, they would come to a point in the river to check on us as we went by them. We stopped for the night in Bamba. A crazy man well known in this town would go on the boats at night and throw objects overboard, so we did not get much sleep with him prowling around us.

The next day we headed out again with the goal of reaching Gao. Before reaching Gao, we encountered an entire family of hippos, and they lunged at us as we passed. This actually created quite a wave that hit our boat. When we got to Gao, we refueled and spent time with the Zimmermans and of course Frank and Eleanor. We left Gao and made it to Ansongo, where we slept on the floor of Ibrima Maiga's house. He was the son of Attino Maiga, the evangelist who preached with us in villages along the river. The next morning we made it to the Mali-Niger border. At the border were rapids. In fact, that is how the border was defined. While going through customs, we asked for a guide to take us through the roaring whitewater. They gave us a young boy to pilot us.

We set off from the shore and within moments were bobbing up and down in the tumbling waters. We immediately disappeared from Frank's view, and he had no idea whether we were still afloat. The boy hollered that I should lift the motor so that it would not hit the rocks. I said, "If I lift it, I will not be able to steer the boat." As we had this exchange, we hit a boulder and got hung up. Bob jumped out to lift it. I told him to jump in quick because as soon as he freed us, we would be headed downstream and he would be left on the rock. Bob jumped on just in time. Within a few moments, our engine did indeed hit a rock, which popped the engine up out of the water. Now we were helplessly riding the rapids—out of control—at the mercy of the river. We were thrust toward a big hippo that opened his mouth to threaten us. The kids were petrified, and so was the adult, especially with the responsibility for the children on board. Again, the *hand of the Lord* guided us when our young guide couldn't. Eventually the river calmed, and we regrouped and got the engine working again and gave thanks that the Lord protected us through rough waters. That night we slept out on a sand dune under the brilliant, starry sky. But even there we were never sure if crocodiles, poisonous snakes, or other dangers lurked around us. We lost contact with Frank. He still didn't know if we had survived the rapids. About 3:00 PM in the afternoon, our mission plane was up looking for us. They saw us just as we approached the mission station.

My closest brush with death along the river happened years later in Gao. The river was very low, so I decided to take a photo of it. While I was adjusting my camera and looking through the lens, I heard the people on the dock start to scream at me. I assumed that they merely did not want me to take a photo. I finally looked up and was stunned to see a huge bull charging full speed with his head down and his long horns aimed directly at me. I had no time to run, and he hit me square between the horns. I thought a horn would skewer me, but there was enough room between the horns for me, and I literally took the bull by the horns. As I hung on to the horns I was running backward, as I was carried along by this angry monster. The Lord gave me the strength to launch myself off the horns, spin to the side, and run like mad while the bull charged ahead without me. Dr. Billy Martin witnessed all of this, and Billy called to me, saying, "Would you do that again so I can get a picture?" That photo would have been worth some money. I didn't have to go to Spain to know what it was like to run with the bulls. I was sore for the next few days, but the Lord was upon me or the bull or both.

Three months prior to our first furlough in 1955, we were joined in the ministry by my brother Frank and his wife, Eleanor. The last three months of our first term were spent in Niger doing construction projects, along with Steve and Louise Black, a great missionary couple. Our first project was to cover the old McCaba house with a new roof. The old roof was a mud roof supported with palm logs. These served as joists, and they were overlaid with old flattened fifty-five-gallon fuel barrels. By now galvanized corrugated metal was available, and steel I beams were sold in the city. We secured I beams, built up the end walls and interior walls with concrete blocks, and set the beams, tying them down securely with reinforcing rods deep down into the walls. We also poured a reinforced concrete cap on top of the roofing over the "I" beams, as tornadoes are frequent in this area, as well as very high winds. While working on this project, a scorpion stung my finger as I picked up a cement block. Even with morphine it was very painful for several days, but as with most scorpion bites, it was not deadly.

After building a garage and storage room in Niamey for our field director, Bob Richards, we added five classrooms to the Christian school that had been developed that year. The steel corrugated roof was so hot that Steve and I decided to fry an egg on it. It took time, but it did cook. Today this school has an enrollment of more than five hundred students, most of whom come from Islamic homes, but as a private school, they are taught by Christian teachers. Bible is a part of their curriculum, and many have trusted Christ as their Savior. It is completely under national leadership, and the students have the highest scholastic rating in Niger.

Four years and seven months had gone by since we had left the States on December 2, 1950, and it was time for our first furlough. My brother Frank and his wife replaced us and took care of the bookstore in our absence.

Chapter 8.
First Furlough

And when they were come, and had gathered the church together, they rehearsed all that God had done with them, and how he had opened the door of faith unto the Gentiles. Acts 14:27

We flew from Niamey to Paris in a DC4 with a stop in Marseilles for refueling. From Paris, we boarded a train to LeHarve, where we boarded the S.S. *United States*, a brand-new ship. This gave us five or six days of rest, between bouts of sea sickness, and lots of good food when we were up to eating. The highlight was getting our first glimpse of the Statue of Liberty off in the distance. As we passed by, we felt a sense of pride in being an American and returning to the "Land of the Free." The pilot had boarded and guided us slowly up the Hudson River to our berth. It was now about 9:00 AM on a Saturday morning. We had completed our breakfast, and all five of us had saved a beautiful orange to eat later in the day, only to find that when we disembarked from the ship, the immigration service confiscated all the fruit, as it was forbidden to take it ashore.

To our surprise, nearly the same crowd of people we left on the dock four and a half years earlier was there again to welcome us home. We assume they went home during the interval! Dave Jr. was reintroduced to his grandparents, uncles, aunts, and cousins. Sandy and Diane had never met any of them. As we walked to the end of the pier, we noticed vendors selling fresh orange juice!

We traveled by car to Bridgeport, Pennsylvania. We were quite a caravan. At lunchtime our chauffer asked if we would like to stop at

McDonalds for lunch. We looked at each other trying to recall who we knew by the name of McDonald, and would they be expecting us? As we approached a town in New Jersey, we noticed the big golden arches. We had no idea what they represented, but this is where we were introduced to McDonalds. A hamburger was fifteen cents, and a cheeseburger was seventeen cents. We felt like we were being treated like royalty.

Arriving back in the States had some challenges, like where would we live? Fortunately, it was summer, and the clothes we wore in Africa would work, although the children were growing, and none of us had shoes, as in Africa we just wore sandals. Shoes in Africa, at least in the desert, were impractical, as they would fill up with sand as you walked and would cramp your feet. The Lord was so good, and He provided sufficient funds for us to go shopping and outfit ourselves with a brand-new wardrobe. We stayed for about two months with Elaine's folks, George and Alberta Beswick. Around Labor Day, we moved to upstate New York, where we moved in with my parents, James and Emily Marshall. They lived in Broadalbin. Dave Jr. or Butch, as he was known, began school there. We were always more than welcome to stay with our parents, but it was not the best situation for them or for us.

We became aware of apartments that were available for furloughing missionaries in Ventnor, New Jersey, called the "Houses of Fellowship." We applied, and one became available to us in January 1956. The Houses of Fellowship consisted of at least thirty apartments located just off of the boardwalk. Several of the apartments had an ocean view. These were provided free of charge, including utilities. There was a playground, tennis courts, and recreation facilities inside and out. They were beautifully furnished. We were almost afraid to move in with three kids who had lived their entire lives in a mud house with a mud roof and some cement and some mud floors. The kids could relate to the sandy beach about one hundred yards away, but this desert was bordered by an ocean. These beautiful facilities were a gift by Mrs. Doane, who was the daughter of William Howard Doane, who composed the music to hundreds of hymns, many of which were written by Fanny Crosby. Mrs. Doane contributed several million dollars to Christian schools, missions, and organizations. The Association of Baptists for World Evangelism began in her home, and she was its first treasurer.

Furlough was not a time for rest but a time to report to our supporting churches and to raise additional support. In the '50s "round robin" missionary conferences were the norm. This was when seven to nine churches would go together, each having an eight-day conference, usually from Sunday to Sunday. Each missionary spoke in a different church each night, and on Sunday in a different church morning and evening. Often on Saturday night was a youth rally with all the young people coming together for a big missionary rally. These were popular in western Pennsylvania, Ohio, Michigan, Indiana, and New York. We slept in a different home each night and ate our meals in different homes. The meetings were well attended, and we met many new people, but by the end of the conference, the missionaries were exhausted. Living on the east coast, we were usually a long way from home at the end of the conference. I usually opted to drive home after the last service, stopping occasionally for a "catnap" or until the cold woke me up. I remember in one month I had meetings scheduled at Saint Joe's Baptist Church, near Fort Wayne, Indiana, Saint Mary's Baptist Church in Saint Mary, Illinois, Saint John's By the Sea in Ventnor, New Jersey, Saint Mary's Methodist Church in Paterson, New Jersey, and Saint Luke's Reformed Episcopal Church in Philadelphia, Pennsylvania. I never published that schedule, as I was a missionary under an approved agency of the General Association of Regular Baptists churches, which frowned upon this. I knew I would spend the rest of my life answering unwanted letters if my preaching in these churches became widely known. But by the time anyone reads this, the Lord may have called me home and I will have already met many people from these churches in glory!

We had a meeting scheduled for a Tuesday evening at a Baptist church in Corinth, New York. It was wintertime, and my dad had loaned us his car. Upon arriving, we were surprised to see that the church was dark and locked. The marquee in front of the church had no mention of a special meeting. The pastor had apparently forgotten that he scheduled us to speak. We headed back to my parents' with the three kids in the backseat, each vying for a seat by the window even though it was pitch dark. In those days, car seats and seat belts did not exist. We felt a sudden rush of cold air and heard a scream. Sandy, who was not yet four years old, had fallen out of the driver's side back door. We slammed on the brakes and looked back in horror as she rolled on the pavement in her yellow snowsuit with headlights of an oncoming car approaching. That car passed right over Sandy and kept on going, but the wheels didn't run over her. I ran and picked her up. She was covered with blood but conscious. At that very spot along this country road there was a tavern. I carried her into the tavern and called an ambulance. We wrapped towels around her bleeding head and ankles while we waited for the ambulance to arrive. The snowsuit protected her body. Sandy's head began to swell to what seemed like twice its normal size. After thirty-six stitches and a lot of bandages, Sandy was released that night from the hospital. The next day we took her to a family physician. He was enraged that the hospital would release her with such swelling. The car that ran over her was high enough to clear the little bundle of love. Again we witnessed the *hand of the Lord.*

The year of furlough went by quickly, and I missed being away from family so much, but with a son in school and two preschool daughters, it was not possible for Elaine to go on these extended trips. We were always thankful when meetings could be scheduled for a weekend that was within one hundred miles so we could go as a family.

God was so good in meeting our needs and the additional support that was required. We chose to return to Africa on a freighter for two reasons. First, we were exhausted from the heavy schedule of deputation, packing, and saying good-bye to family and friends, and second, we were allowed three hundred pounds of baggage per person on the ship or fifteen hundred compared to forty-four pounds per person by plane or a total of 220 pounds for a family of five. The ten days or more at sea would be restful, relaxing, and a great family time.

We left New York with a host of family and friends to see us off on a beautiful summer day. We sailed to Halifax, Nova Scotia, where we took on tons of wheat and flour. From there, our next stop was the Azores Islands, where we anchored in a bay and unloaded cargo onto a barge. A small launch came alongside to take us to shore. Each of us donned life jackets as we literally had to jump into the launch because of the rough sea, and the launch just bobbed up and down alongside of the gangway.

The Azores were very primitive, with few vehicles. Most transport was by oxcart. We understood that the average worker earned less than a dollar a day. We came across a cemetery, which we walked through, noticing the skeletal remains of deceased persons laying on top of the graves exposed to the sun and weather, with the bones picked clean by the gulls. We inquired about this and were told that the Catholic church owned the cemetery and that the graves are rented, and if families defaulted on their payments, the remains were then removed from the grave. The grave was then rented to another family for burial and the original occupant was simply laid exposed on top of the grave.

Upon returning to the ship, the launch was unable to get close to the ship because of the waves, and thus the longshoreman helped us get from the launch to the barge. The ship could not lower the gangway, fearing that it would get crushed between the barge and the ship. Thus they decided to put the five of us in a cargo net that had a wooden pallet in the center. The ship's boom would lift the net and then swing us on board over the deck and lower us down to safety. This was an experience none of us would ever forget, especially since the sun had already disappeared and it was pitch dark except for a floodlight from the ship's mast. Soon the ship's whistle blew, signaling that our cargo had all been loaded onto the barge and that we were getting underway.

Having left New York ten days earlier, we were now along the west coast of Africa, and Dakar came into view. Dakar was quite modern. We stayed overnight in a cheap hotel, and the next day we made arrangements to take the train that linked the landlocked French Sudan to the coast. The distance between Dakar and Bamako was over thirteen hundred kilometers. We obtained first-class tickets, which gave us padded seats, which converted into sleeping bunks at night. The trip was supposed to last about twenty hours but turned out to be twenty-eight hours. This was the rainy season, and there were mechanical breakdowns and washouts. The railroad was a narrow gauge, and they were in the process of welding the track together and then stretching it to compensate for expansion and contraction.

The scenery between Dakar and Bamako was pretty much the same, with reddish-orange laterite soil dotted with scrub thorn bushes. Much of West Africa is orange and green. Maybe it is no accident these colors are found in most flags of West African nations. The engine was a diesel that had replaced the steam engines. The former steam engines were fueled by wood, which was cut along the tracks. Soon the forests were depleted, and so wood had to be transported on the backs of donkeys to designated depots where the train would stop to refuel.

At Bamako, we took a taxi to the Gospel Missionary Union headquarters, where Lloyd McRostie and his wife provided housing and meals for us. Being the rainy season, it was extremely humid as well as hot, and almost immediately we all broke out with "prickly heat." In Bamako, we spent the next few days shopping for canned food, powdered milk, cooking gas, and other things not available in Timbuktu. We had to pack it up and ship it on the riverboat to Koriome. We did not own a vehicle, so this was a lot of walking in the hot sun. Soon we would be ready for the last part of our journey to Timbuktu with our three children, ages seven, four, and two and a half.

Timbuktu was one thousand kilometers from Bamako. There was the weekly Air France flight to Goundam, but without scheduled ground transportation, you had to hope that a military truck had come to the airport and that the driver would be kind enough to make room for your family and luggage for the trip to Timbuktu. He also would take the mail and provisions that the army had ordered from the capital and of course military passengers arriving on the plane.

We opted to take the riverboat (*The Archinard*), which was a five-day trip down the Niger River. This gave us an opportunity to relax and rest for a few days, plus have our baggage and provisions with us. This riverboat was brand new, with nice accommodations. It had four classes. First class had two single beds in each cabin, which was located on the second deck on the forward half of the boat. Back in the '50s the only people who traveled in first class were French functionaries working for the government, tourists, and Lebanese merchants. Second class was on the back half of the second deck, with four beds for each cabin. Third class was in a large room on the main deck, and fourth class was just on the deck anywhere there was room to roll down a mat. On the third deck was a nice dining room for the first class. At the back on the second class level was a dining room for second class. The third class just had several large bowls of rice provided African style with no dishes or silverware with about eight people sharing each bowl of rice.

The riverboat also carried up to 150 tons of cargo below the main deck. There wasn't any limit to the number of passengers in fourth class. The other three classes were limited by the number of beds. The kitchen was located on the main deck, and the crew lived forward in the bow and aft in the stern. They did their cooking on open wood fires on deck. Their stove consisted of a clay bowl with protruding three-clay prongs on which they would set either an aluminum pot or a clay pot containing their food. Between the three prongs they inserted a piece of wood that burned well, as there was always a breeze from the movement of the boat. I refer to this as a boat, for when I was in the navy, we were instructed that a boat was a vessel that could be hoisted onto a ship. I'm sure this "riverboat" was too large to be put onto a ship, but then I've never heard of a river ship, as they are always referred to as a riverboat.

We had stops at all major towns along the river. These stops provided the
passengers in fourth class an opportunity to buy food. The shore was dotted with vendors with large wooden bowls or gourds filled with milk

(along with a more than a few drowned flies floating on top), chicken that had been boiled in deep fat (usually peanut oil), pieces of beef, goat, or sheep, bread, and coffee. Just watching these merchants was worth the price of the ticket.

Chapter 9.

Back Home in Timbuktu

...let us go again and visit our brethren in every city where we have preached the word of the Lord, and see how they do.
Acts 15:36

After five relaxing days on the Niger River, we finally arrived early in the morning at Koriome. My brother Frank and his family had already left for furlough, so there was no one to meet us. This was not a problem, as there were always plenty of people, both French and nationals, alike who came to meet the boat. The boat was a lifeline for Europeans who lived along the river.

The boat crew had quite a business going. They would buy oranges, limes, pineapples, mangoes, and potatoes in Bamako to sell to the people in the desert. None of these things were available to people in the north. One gentleman on the boat who was just under the *"Commisaire"* had the privilege of using the cold room on the boat, so he had a business of buying up butter, cheese, salami, and other food that required refrigeration. He sold it to the white expatriates along the river at a great profit.

It was good to be home and visit with our landlord, Kader Gornia, and old Baba, who now was nearly blind. He lived across the alleyway from us. He always enjoyed our kids. He was an old mason and was still able to cut alhor. He would chop it into square blocks with his machete. It would then be used to face the mud buildings, usually on the east side. It was laid up in mud and then pointed with cement. The driving rains (the few that we got) came from the east, and the cement protected the walls from erosion.

The first job was to fill the kerosene refrigerator and light the wick, and then send Touridya for water and get our filter working for drinking water, and then house cleaning. Everything was covered with sand and dirt.

While we had been on furlough, Bill and Lois Carmichael arrived on the field. Their first year was spent in Gao, and then they opened up a new ministry in the town of Niafunke up river from Timbuktu about 175 kilometers.

Elaine and I concentrated on both regular services in Timbuktu as well as villages along the river. The local chiefs were cooperative and would call their people together for the first hearing, but the local *marabouts,* or Muslim teachers, would often get up and walk away, sometimes taking half of our congregation with him. Elaine would teach the women, but often a man was standing by and would say it was impossible for a woman to understand. All of these women and men were illiterate, which made it more difficult. We had nowhere to stay in these villages, and with three small children and mosquito infestation along the river, we began to realize two things. First, people who already have their religion and faithfully practice it probably are not going to respond to the gospel after one hearing, and we could not return often enough to make a positive impact to a hostile group who not only practiced their religion but also defended it. The realization was that we should spend our time ministering in Timbuktu, where we could develop friendships, trust, and rapport and have quality time with people. Timbuktu also offered the advantage of having schools, and at least 25 percent of the people were literate. We began to think of a compromise—a house boat that would be a floating mission station.

Although many were illiterate, we observed that local people had tremendous memories. They could recite from memory their personal genealogies back hundreds of years, perhaps because traditionally they were an oral culture, learning by listening to stories and teachings, rather than by reading books. Some adults had memorized long sections of the Koran. We noticed that the children easily learned the books of the Bible forward and backward, and they even could stop in the middle and go either way. Adults and children memorized Scripture easily and quickly.

Physical Challenges

During this time, we were trying to grow a vegetable garden during our cool season. I had a small centrifugal pump, and we had a well on the property that the C&MA had turned over to us. There was no electricity, but we had a small gasoline engine that ran our Maytag washing machine. I adapted the pump to the engine and mounted them on a piece of three-quarter-inch plywood. The problem was that the pump could push water, but would only lift it about eleven feet. To test it out, I took the pump with a garden hose attached to it to the bottom of the well, being assisted by Touridya to lower me fifty feet down into the three-and-a-half-foot-wide well. I started the engine and was waiting anxiously for Elaine to tell me when the water was coming out. But my body was beginning to tingle, and it felt like pins and needles. I didn't realize it, but I was being overcome with carbon monoxide gas. I was barely conscious.

Touridya, thank God, was strong, and I only weighed 150 pounds. He was able to pull me up fifty feet out of the well with the help of a pulley attached to the rope. I laid on the ground breathing with great difficulty. The French doctor was gone, but the *"Medecin African,"* who had three years of medical training, was at the clinic a quarter of a mile away. He came quickly. There was no oxygen at the clinic. He began immediately giving me artificial respiration. He did this for about a half hour. Dr. Daouda sent a male nurse home with me, who stayed all night, and about every ten minutes he gave me artificial respiration throughout the night. (Recently my nephew, Bob Marshall, recounted that a man in Segou, Mali, told him that he was there when I was pulled from the well fifty years prior.) This was my first near-death experience in West Africa, but it would not be the last. During that night, Elaine didn't know if I was going to make it. While weakened from the episode, God provided strength in the months that followed.

Later, Elaine became very ill with congestion on her lungs, probably pneumonia, and Dr. Pincon ordered her to be evacuated one thousand kilometers to Point G, the largest hospital in Mali just outside of Bamako. The French army provided an old WWII Dodge ambulance for the trip over a rough sand track that followed a telephone line the 115 kilometers across the desert to Goundam for the weekly Air France flight. A male nurse and I accompanied her. God provided a couple who volunteered to care for our children, Monsieur and Madame Dejoux. Air France had taken seats out of the twin-engine DC 3 and replaced them with a cot so that Elaine would be in a horizontal position. The nurse sat next to Elaine, and I had a seat in front of the nurse. After making stops at Mopti and Segou, we landed in Bamako and were met by an ambulance, which transported us to the hospital.

This was Monday, and the next flight back to Goundam would be on Saturday. I stayed at the Gospel Missionary Union (GMU) mission and walked each morning to the Grand Hotel a couple miles away where taxis, would take me up the mountain to the hosptial. I did this both morning and afternoon. Elaine was receiving good care and seemed to be responding well to the medication. It was decided that I return home to care for the children and someone from GMU mission would visit Elaine each day. During the five days that I was in Bamako and walking in the hot sun I did not realize what was happening in my own body. My strength was gone, and I was very weak. On Saturday morning, I boarded the plane going to Goundam, making the two stops between. The heat in the plane seemed unbearable, especially on the ground. There was no air conditioning in the DC 3, and by noon the plane bounced like a kite out of control going up and down, plus about half of the twenty-eight passengers were throwing up, and the stench was intolerable. Goundam's airstrip had no buildings. It was 1:00 PM, and the sun was baking us. After the passengers, freight, and mail going to Goundam and Timbuktu were taken off the plane, the plane taxied down the runway, where it would turn at the end. I could not see the plane, as it was followed by dust. After the dust settled, I could hear the pilot rev up engine one, followed by engine two, and then the take off. Again the cloud of dust trailed, and eventually the plane lifted off, the wheels were retracted, and it was on its way to Gao, where it would overnight. On Sunday. it would go to Niamey in Niger and returning back to Gao by nightfall. On Monday it would return to Goundam, Mopti, Segou, and Bamako.

I bummed a ride with a military truck in Goundam. The trucks were old World War II leftovers, so we waited until about 6:00 PM before leaving, as the radiator would overheat during the hottest part of the day. The first stop was the post office in Timbuktu. Getting out of the truck in front of the post office, I tried to get my suitcase and fell to the ground exhausted with a heat stroke.

Our children were in the house next to the post office where the DeJouxs lived. The next thing I knew, Dr. Pincon was leaning over me. I was completely dehydrated. Soon I had four bottles of saline solution going in me, one in each arm and one in each leg. I was told my children were there, but I don't remember seeing them or being able to talk or kiss them. David was seven, Sandy four, and Diane three. The DeJouxs did not speak English. David spoke some French, but Sandy and Diane could not communicate with their caretakers and had not seen or heard from Mom and Dad for a week. Now Dad is there but unable to hug them or talk to them. I was bedridden for a week in the home of the Dejouxs. Dr. Pincon by now realized that he couldn't help me and was fearful that I would not make it. He pleaded with the French air force to send a plane to Timbuktu to evacuate me. He knew I could not survive the trip to Goundam. Within several hours, a plane could be heard circling over Timbuktu, and I was put into the ambulance and driven to the dirt runway. Soon I heard the plane on the ground.

Apparently the plane must have refueled in Mopti on its way north, as we went nonstop from Timbuktu to Bamako. We were met by an ambulance at Bamako. The next problem we would incur was that when we arrived at the hospital all of the African staff had gone on strike and I was left unable to get out of the ambulance lying in the hot sun. Finally, several French nurses came and carried me on a stretcher, not only into the building but upstairs. I'm not sure how long I was there before I was able to explain that my wife was a patient in the next building and I wanted to know how she was doing. After a day, they verified my story and carried me to the next building and put me in the same room with her. The next day, some missionaries from GMU came to visit Elaine, and when they entered the room, they were shocked that they had put a man in the same room with her. I was unrecognizable, as I had not shaved for over two weeks and my hair was not combed. Within minutes, Elaine was able to explain who I was and why I was there. Within about ten days, we were released on condition that we go somewhere where we would have complete rest.

We checked into the Lido Hotel, a small hotel a few miles out of the capital. We immediately sent a telegram to Timbuktu requesting that our children be brought to Bamako. While Elaine and I were in the hospital in Bamako, our mission had arranged to send a missionary couple to Timbuktu to care for our children. This couple had no children of their own and no experience in child care. When we met our kids at the airport, it was obvious that they had been mistreated. Diane, three years old, had bruises on her bottom, and all three were nervous wrecks. Our children's mother and father had been evacuated, and they were left with total strangers. The kids had no idea where we were and felt abandoned. Diane had been beaten for wetting her pants. Then if she wet her pants, she would try to hide them to avoid another spanking, which only doubled her punishment. To add insult to real injuries, this couple dumped our pet lynx out in the middle of the desert in front of the children on the way to the Goundam airport. God, in His love, never gave this couple children of their own. A year later, the man was killed in an accident.

At the hotel there was a swimming pool fed by a creek that came down from the mountain. We all enjoyed refreshing ourselves from the heat. The Lido also had a bottling plant where they bottled pop in different flavors, orange, lime, and grenadine (Coca-Cola still had not yet been introduced to this part of Africa). Having pop was a big deal for us too! Our girls have never acquired a taste for carbonated drinks to this day.

Getting Well in Guinea

While at this hotel, we learned of a missionary couple from GMU who were leaving the field, and they offered to sell us their four-wheel drive Willys pick-up truck. We arranged to get enough for a down payment and paid the remainder over the next year. The GMU had a vacation house at Delaba in the neighboring colony of Guinea, located high in the cool-forested mountains. It was not being used for a month and was offered to us. So now owning our first vehicle in Africa, we took a vacation in Guinea.

The guesthouse was four cement block walls and a tin roof. There was no bathroom but a three hole outhouse. This was amusing to Butch who immediately asked, "Why three holes? Does everyone go to the toilet together?" I still do not have the answer to that, unless it was a precaution for the kids in case there were snakes that took shelter in the privy.

We enjoyed our family time together, especially hiking to a very high waterfall that was wide but just a thin sheet of water, which allowed the kids to run under and behind it without being knocked down. Thousands of beautiful tropical butterflies fluttered around the paths and roadsides. On our walk back to the cabin, we noticed an army of large ants that had built their own road in what looked like tar. Unfortunately, Sandy stepped on their road, and she was immediately attacked by hundreds of biting ants and she began to scream. These ants, biting furiously, had a way of clinging to her with no mercy. Finally we were able to get all the ants off, but she was in pain and quite swollen for another day as these ants, apparently venomous, had bites like bee stings.

After three weeks, we were anxious to get back to work. The roads in Guinea were terrible—almost impassible—and very dangerous. In the mountains, the roads had cliffs on one side and sheer escarpments on the other. There were many hair-pin turns and often log bridges in the middle of the turn. Often the bridges were out, and it required stopping and rebuilding them to get across the mountain streams. The prudent thing was to drive in the mountains at night, because you could see the headlights of oncoming traffic, especially at the turns, whereas in the daylight there is no warning. When it rained, the road was like driving on ice. Once we slid about fifty feet with our brakes locked down, a mountain cliff was on our left side and we were completely out of control. There was no guard rail! God was good to us, and we arrived safely in Bamako.

The next day we spent buying supplies that we would need in Timbuktu, like powdered milk and cereal, as well as supplies for the trip. It would be about seven hundred miles of which 400 miles would be in the desert with no road and in an area where we had never traveled. We loaded the truck with gas, plus an extra fifty-five-gallon barrel of gas, and a couple of jerry cans each with five gallons of gas. We had a galvanized five-gallon jerry can of filtered drinking water, plus a heavy canvas jug that held another three gallons of water. I had purchased two cases of soda pop, each with twenty-four bottles. Elaine and the two girls sat on the front seat along with me; Butch rode in the back with the supplies, gasoline, suitcases, and other cargo. His seat was on powdered milk cases, but in rough areas, he would stand, holding on to the barrel of gasoline.

We arrived in Kemacina along the side of the Niger River, where we stayed in a *campement* over night. I reported to the commandant that evening and informed him that we would be leaving early in the morning. Vehicles were warned to check in and report their intentions of driving across the desert so the commander could advise the next commander by radio that someone was coming. Only one or two vehicles a month would take this difficult trip. During the night, we had a hard rain storm.

As planned, we left early in the morning, and after going for an hour or two, we left the sand tracks and came to a large mud flat that was partially flooded. I stopped and turned my front wheel caps to engage us into four-wheel drive. Cautiously, we entered the mud, and after going about seventy-five feet, our four wheels were all turning, and we were at a standstill. The more we tried to go, the deeper we sank. Elaine and I, knowing we were in deep mud and there was no one in sight, decided to get out, but I took my trousers off and Elaine took her skirt off to keep from getting them muddy. We scoured around looking in vain for something to put under the wheels to give us traction. I did have a few tools and decided to take the tailgate off and use it as a footing to put the jack on to try to lift one wheel at a time out of the mud hole and put under them branches from scrub bushes that we could find under the wheels to give us traction.

It was May, and the temperatures were scorching hot—maybe as high as 140 degrees. After about two hours of wallowing like pigs in the mud, we were ready to give it a shot. Our next concern was that everything that grows in the desert is loaded with thorns we did not need any flat tires. We climbed in the pick-up, and we slowly began to move forward, and praise the Lord, we were out of the mud. We stopped, put the tailgate back on, put the jack back behind the seat, and continued on our way.

My legs were covered with mud to my thighs, so for the next hour, I drove in my underwear. Driving in the desert in the sunlight is very difficult, as you cannot see the bumps or washouts, as the sun is directly overhead and there are no shadows. Then we hit a bump and the fifty-five-gallon drum bounced up and came down, pinning Butch's sandal under it, but just missing his toes. God is so good. His toes could have been severed. As I got out of the truck, I found that all of the mud had dried on my legs and was attaching itself to every hair on my legs. "Ouch, Ouch!" I screamed. As I was stretching my legs from the seated position, I tore all the hair off from my legs.

After lashing down the drum and the cases, I put my trousers back on over the dried mud and got back in the seat and tried to start the engine. Not a sound. Apparently the starter went out on it. The guy I bought the vehicle from had made a hand crank, but he must not have used it, because it did not fit. I was not a mechanic and it was noontime; we were baking in the hot Sahara sun. We were in deep sand, with no way to push, no hill to go down so I could try to throw it into gear to start it. We were in the middle of nowhere. Off in the distance, I saw a shepherd. I blew the horn, but there was no response. We huddled into what little shade the vehicle would give, aware that vehicles seldom traveled this road. Our small children and Elaine and I were already exhausted from the previous episode in mud. We began to pray and asked the Lord to help us. We had already expended a lot of our water. Our girls hated carbonated drinks, so Elaine, Butch, and I consumed a lot of it. We needed the sugar as we were physically exhausted.

After about an hour, we began to hear the noise of an engine. Was it on the ground or in the air? Soon it was apparent it was on the ground, and it was God's miracle taking care of His dumb sheep. The vehicle was a French Renault Caravan similar to a Chevy Carryall loaded with about twelve husky men, some nomads, others black Songhai. They stopped, and after explaining our problem, they all went to the back of our pick up and began to push in the deep, hot sand. We did not go far when I threw it into gear and the engine ignited and began to purr. We thanked them profusely, and they went on their way, and we went our way in opposite directions. The *hand of the Lord* again provided help in a time of need.

After about a half hour, we arrived in the village of Lere, very close to the border of Mauritania. There was a well there, and people were drawing water. Elaine and I shed a couple pounds of mud as we bathed right there at the well. I refused to turn the key off and let the engine run. No one had any air conditioning in those days either in their cars or in homes, even where electricity was available in the capital cities. After bathing and feeling refreshed and the kids being able to run a little, we continued on our way all night long toward Niafunke.

When we arrived in Niafunke, we stayed in the *campement* overnight. This was a larger village, and I was sure I could get plenty of manpower if I needed it for a push. I shut the engine down, and in the morning, the engine started up, and we never had it happen again. I went to visit the commander in the morning to advise him that we had arrived from Kemacina and his response was simply, "I was not aware that you were coming!" We then left for Timbuktu, passing through Goundam, arriving home about noon in the heat of the day. Thank you, Lord, our eight gallons of drinking water and twenty-four bottles of soda were all gone—not a drop left—but it was enough, and we lived to tell you of God's faithfulness!

TIMBUKTU

Sand dunes with Timbuktu in the background

Our first home with the only round windows in Timbuktu

Our home on the mission station in town

Overview of the city of Timbuktu

Djingareiber (house of prayer) a large mosque built in the 15th century

David on his way to minister in villages along the Niger River

Mohamed Lamin was first known Christian in Timbuktu

View of the port in Timbuktu from our roof top during high water season

Cone well which was dug by hand are terraced for gardens

Sankore Mosque, the site of an Islamic university in the early 15th century

Blocks of salt cut to various sizes in the market

Elaine working at the Christian bookstore

David baptizing Kalifa a soldier who later became a pastor

Our church in Timbuktu, "Eglise Evangelique Baptiste "

Diane and Touridya upon her return to Timbuktu in 1990

Team from Kokomo church lowering a team member into a well to deepen it

Teaching nomads God's word through agriculture

Joe Stowell having coffee break with missionaries and local pastors

Large canoes that carried 30 tons of equipment for the Living Water Project

Installing fence around 60 acres of the Living Water Project to keep livestock out

Lush gardens grow from sandy soil at the Living Water Project

Niger Gospel Boat

Niger Gospel Boat going to dry dock for repairs

Chapter 10.
Building the Mission Station

"The more obstacles you have the more opportunities there are for God to do something." Clarence W. Jones

Our next adventure was building a mission station at Timbuktu. While we had a "permit to occupy" the thirty-by-forty meter piece of land at the southeast corner of the town, we did not want to make an investment in buildings without a clear title. At the same time, we requested an additional thirty-by-forty meter section, giving us a piece thirty-by-eighty meters. To get the clear title, we would have to pay a fee set by the government to an African, who could prove that the land was used as pasture for his animals. This was only about $300. Then there was a fee for the government per square meter, plus the cost of having the land surveyed and corner boundaries set. This all went very smoothly, as the director of the "Service of Domaines" was familiar with our mission in Niger. Within three months, we had all the official documents.

Building materials were scarce, and in order to build on land with a permanent title, it was required to be *"endur,"* which meant built with cement rather than mud. In this part of the Sahara, the sand was so fine, it was like powder, and the closest gravel was 150 kilometers up the river in a river bed called Tondi Farma. There was only one cement building in Timbuktu, and that was the home of the French veterinarian. This was a new structure and was well financed by the government. A vet clinic was also "endure" on the same property. For us to build, it would require several thousand cement blocks. As mentioned, the sand had no grit in it, but the gravel at Tondi Farma was pea size and the sand would be satisfactory as a filler with cement in making blocks. The mission in Niger had a block mold that had been shipped to Gao. I rented a sixty-ton barge from the riverboat company, which they dropped off at Tonka, a market town about five kilometers from Tondi Farma. I hired several men, and we loaded shovels and buckets into my boat. We punched holes in the bottom of the buckets so they would act like a sieve as we put the gravel scraped from the bottom of the river into them. We all got into my outboard motor boat and traveled up the river to Tonka, where we found our barge that had been left there by a tugboat. The tug had continued on toward Gao, with six large barges filled with rice and millet.

We purchased bamboo poles, fastened a rope to the back of my boat, and began to pull and pole the barge toward Tondi Farma. My little "tugboat" was of some help, but the men poling were the biggest help. We anchored the barge in the river, and we all jumped overboard into the river, which was between waist and chest deep. None of us gave any thought about crocodiles that might be looking for a meal. Perhaps our stirring up mud as we scraped up the gravel kept them at bay. Actually, in about eight hours, we filled the barge as much as we dared, as we did not want to sink it. We poled and pulled the barge back to Tonka where we left it until another real tugboat would arrive and pull it to Koriome. At Koriome, we unloaded the gravel onto the shore. I then transported it in the back of my Willys pick-up with about thirty-five or forty trips to our building site. Cement came from France, and fortunately the French subsidized the transport of building materials. The price of a bag of cement was about 20 percent higher than the cost of a bag in the United States, a bargain when you consider the normal cost of transport.

Prior to starting the construction of our residence, the government was going to build a small, seven-room hotel in Timbuktu, along with a dining room and bar. The plan was to construct it out of burned clay tiles that were fabricated in Segou. When they arrived, the contractor refused to accept them because they were misshaped. Later we purchased some of these deformed bricks to build our small chapel and classroom. This room was eight feet by thirteen feet. It was used for about twenty years for our chapel and Bible classes throughout the week. It took a whole ton of cement to plaster the inside of the building, which had four small windows and a plywood door. Our cement bricks for the residence and garage/storeroom were individually made with a block mold.

This mission station is still there and served missionary families well for several decades. We have mentioned that time seems to stand still in Timbuktu, and this mission station is evidence of that phenomenon. Diane had left Mali in 1970 (more on that later), and when she returned with her husband twenty years later in 1990, the mission station had all of the same furniture, utensils, dishes, metal glasses, and even the same towels were being used that had her name sewn in them! It was as if she never left.

Visitors

We hosted many visitors in the mission station over the years. Mr. "Soapy" Williams—undersecretary of state for African affairs—and his wife were two of our visitors. He was a former Michigan governor and part of the family that owned the Mennen-Williams Aftershave company. When the African officials heard that he was coming, they feverishly tried to clean up the town and put up decorations. They knew that the American flag was red, white, and blue, so they put up a British flag. Then below that they put up an American flag, but they hung it upside down. They had dinner with us, and we got to know these very nice, down-to-earth folks.

Leopold Sangar, the first president of Senegal and a poet, visited Timbuktu. The local authorities always put a platform up, and all foreigners would be asked to sit on the platform with the honored guest to greet him and shake his hand. At this time, Americans were not liked, as Mali was a socialist country aligned with the Soviet Union, but when President Bourgiba of Tunisia came to visit, he shook my hand and said, "I am so glad there is an American here! I was sure surprised, but maybe I shouldn't have been." His son was the Tunisian ambassador to the United States. Felix Houphouët-Boigny—the first president of Ivory Coast, who held that office for thirty-three years—came up to Timbuktu with a huge entourage on two riverboats filled with people, including his cabinet. The president of Mali and his cabinet escorted him, so we had two presidents there at once. I was asked to use my boat to rescue some government officials whose boat had broken down while they were rounding up villagers to be present to welcome the leaders. I picked up the government workers, and together we spread the word about the presidents' arrival in Timbuktu. Yet in spite of those efforts, we somehow were not on the guest list for the formal dinner. We were friends with the chauffer of the head of the national assembly. He stopped by, and I teased him, saying, "How can you ask me to go help your officials and round up all the people to come and I don't get an invitation to the dinner?"

After their visit, they went on to Gao, and then we learned that they were going to return to Timbuktu for "an intimate dinner." We did get an invitation to this intimate dinner. An old man who was a veteran of WWII had been left off the previous list, as well as another missionary couple, so all of us were invited to this more intimate dinner. The women all went to the home of a wealthy merchant, and the men went to another home. At the women's party, there was quite a scene, as all of the women of Timbuktu wore (and still wear) long skirts, but Houphouët-Boigny's wife aspired to be a modern western woman and had worn a tight mini-skirt. All of the other women sat on the floor, as was the custom, but the first lady of the Ivory Coast couldn't sit with that skirt, and so they got her a chair. The mix of socialites and local women made for quite an entertaining evening. At our meeting, we were eating in typical fashion sitting around a large bowl and everybody digging in with their hands out of that bowl.

Houphouët-Boigny's wife was known as the Jackie Kennedy of Africa. She would fly to Paris on weekends to get her hair done. Her husband was one of the wealthiest men in the world. He later built the world's largest Basilica, as well as a large mosque and a Protestant church, to cover all the faiths, along with an opulent palace, university, hotel, and Congress building all in his home town, and he even moved the capital to what was once a humble village.

Occasionally, we got to visit dignitaries on their turf. It would not always go well for us missionaries. For example, after Malian Independence, the United States opened an embassy in Bamako. Every Fourth of July, the ambassador would invite all of us Americans to an American-style picnic. The embassy had many things that the rest of us never had access to in Mali. For example, they had hot dogs, which, as you can imagine, are hard to find in an Islamic country. At one of these picnics, a dear old missionary who had served the Lord many years in Mali took a hot dog and put it in her purse. When she left, she forgot her purse. The embassy staff had to go through her purse to identify who it belonged to, and of course, it was very embarrassing for her and everybody involved when they found the hidden hotdog.

In 1957, America's foremost newscaster and documentary producer, Lowell Thomas, came to Timbuktu accompanied by ten cinematographers to make a film for *High Adventure*, which were specials run at primetime on TV. There was no hotel yet in Timbuktu, so we got to know this humble, down-to-earth gentleman well by inviting him for meals. He included us in the documentary, which was quite a Hollywood production. They staged an attack by the Tuaregs with the swords and spears raiding a camel caravan. During one scene, they had to cover up the word Dodge on the military trucks used in the film because the show was sponsored by GM. He was a fascinating man who had interviewed Lawrence of Arabia prior to WWI and was very much involved in bringing fame to Lawrence of Arabia and in making the Lawrence of Arabia film. On our next furlough, we met Lowell in New York City, and at his invitation joined him for a private showing of the film titled, *From Madagascar to Timbuktu* in his acclaimed *High Adventure* series.

Throughout the mission compound-building process, I constantly felt tired and weak. I would even have dizzy spells. Meanwhile, Elaine had contracted Hepatitis C, probably while in the hospital. I stayed on until the roof was on the residence and then left the completion of the building to my brother, Frank. Elaine and I decided we needed to return to the States to recuperate. I believe that neither of us had fully recovered from those illnesses that put us together in the hospital.

Chapter 11.

The Niger Gospel Boat

"I have found that there are three stages in every great work of God, first it is impossible, then it is difficult, then it is done."
J. Hudson Taylor

While home on medical leave, I began to design a house boat as a floating mission station. Lowell Thomas, during our meeting in New York City, gave me the name of a boat manufacturer in Gary, Indiana. They had a boat that would accommodate seven people. It had a small gas refrigerator and a gas stove. There were three bunk beds, a couch that opened into a double bed, and the dining room table that lowered between the two benches into another double bed. The cost was $3,500. Where would we get that kind of money? That was the price in Gary, so by the time we would get it to Mali, the price would be double. I presented it to our missionaries, and without exception, all of them wanted to make it a field project. Thinking back to my navy days and having missed by one week being a "plank owner" of the USS *Portsmouth* since I boarded the ship one week after it was commissioned, the thought came about making people who gave $5 or more to become plank owners of the Niger Gospel Boat.

I designed a brochure to mail to our prayer partners and a certificate to send to those who wished to become a plank owner. Each missionary inserted one of these in a letter to their prayer partners. My oldest brother, Gordon, took care of the mailing out of the certificates. The Lord used this promotion, and soon all the funds were supplied. God is so good!

We returned to Africa for our third term as usual on a freighter. We watched with some anxiety as they loaded our boat on the same ship upon which we were travelling. The boat was thirty-five feet long and eight feet wide. Catwalks eighteen inches wide had been cut off and packed inside the hull to be re-welded before launching into the Niger River. As they were lowering it into the freighter's hold, it banged against the opening on the deck and bent the transom, but that was minor damage and repairable.

On arrival at Dakar, we found that the boat would just fit on a flat car of the narrow gauge train. We left it in the hands of a freight forwarder and continued on to Bamako. As always when in Bamako, we had to purchase supplies before going north. We bought ten cases of powdered milk, ten bottles of gas for our stove, and lots of other supplies unavailable in Timbuktu. We shipped these supplies on the riverboat, which arrived in Timbuktu shortly after we did.

After several weeks, we finally received word that the Niger Gospel Boat or *Bonne Nouvelle (Good News)* had arrived in Bamako and the process of clearing it through customs was underway. Our next big job would be to get it shipped sixty kilometers down river to Koulikoro, the river port where we would unpack it and launch it into the river and begin to assemble the cabin. Bill Carmichael joined my brother Frank and I, and we took the Mali riverboat from Timbuktu some nine hundred kilometers to Koulikoro.

At Koulikoro, we took the train to Bamako to take care of the customs paperwork. After traveling about thirty kilometers, I went to the restroom such as it was. In Africa, when you bought a train ticket, there were always three or four copies, with a piece of carbon paper in between each copy of the ticket. The paper had carbon on both sides. Normally restrooms were not provided with toilet paper, but this restroom had a large twenty-penny nail driven through the wall with about one hundred sheets of used carbon paper stuck over the nail. I could hardly contain myself as I looked. I began to laugh, and I called Bill and Frank, and we laughed all the way to Bamako. It was a good way to recycle carbon paper, but for us white people, it left its mark! Our experiences in Africa were a lot of fun, and we remember them with fondness.

We began assembling our boat with the help of Ruben Friesen, a missionary with GMU. Ruben had a Yankee screwdriver (a mechanical one that turned the screw as you pushed in on it), which was a tremendous help and saved us many blisters in driving in hundreds of screws. Packed in the hull, we also had a windmill, water pump, pipes, life jackets, stove, kerosene refrigerator, and tires that we had purchased in the States. While in Koulikoro, I used a $100 gift from a tourist who worked for the World

Bank to buy steel angle iron to make the tower for the windmill. I designed the tower on the ground, laying it out and marking it. The boat company allowed me to use their hydraulic press to punch holes and cut the iron, which was a huge blessing. We might still be working on it if it were not for Ruben's screwdriver and the generous boat company.

With the boat assembled, it was tied to the side of the riverboat and towed to Niafunke, where it was dropped off with Bill and Lois Carmichael. We paid the normal rate for shipping three tons of freight (the weight of the boat) to have it transported in this way. We had three other mission stations along the Niger. Frank and Eleanor Marshall were stationed in Dire, Elaine and I were stationed in Timbuktu, and Dan and Ann Zimmerman were in Gao. We scheduled this floating mission station so that each family had the use of the boat, starting with the Carmichaels as they received the high water first, ending with the Zimmermans in Gao, which received the flood waters last. Each family had the use of it an equal amount of time, and hundreds of villages were reached with the gospel.

We would often preach from the front of the boat. It reminded us of accounts of Jesus preaching from the boat to people on shore. Besides preaching, we had permission from the government to dispense medicine and treat illness along the river. This always attracted a large crowd. Dan Zimmerman had forceps and removed bad teeth. He had a large number ten can that he kept on board with all the teeth he had pulled. Maybe the better term is "extracted." The can was more than half full, and it really stunk. Finally, somebody dumped them out.

During the rice harvest season, many villagers worked in the fields, while others used long sticks to beat out the rice on the threshing floor. By the end of the day, they all came to the boat to get a rub down on their aching backs with a squirt of peanut oil. They would love that! They all came with aching backs to get their backs rubbed. They also got a couple aspirin, which was taken with water from the river in a calabash. Besides the children who were burned from falling into the open cooking fires—a common occurrence—the most common ailments were malaria, eye diseases, dysentery, and infections. We would give antibiotics, eye-drops, or whatever else we had in the way of medicines. Ulcers also were common, and the native treatment was manure, which festered with maggots, which ate the dead flesh. We were always amazed at how fast after a couple days of flushing out the sores and applying compresses of potassium permanganate and bandaging with an antibiotic that healing would take place. Foot injuries were caused by stepping on fish bones, as many people were fisherman and the fish were cleaned along the river's edge and then dried in the sun. Some villages were completely devoid of children under six years old because of an epidemic of measles, causing complications, and the children would die. There were no clinics, doctors, nurses, or medicine available to them. Whooping cough was treated with donkey milk. As mentioned earlier, runny noses were often sucked out by mothers, thus spreading illnesses. We did the best we could, but oh how we longed to have a doctor or nurse on our team!

Butch always had fishing gear and had lots of fish, which also attracted attention of the local villagers. Sometimes the locals would bring us fish—dogfish, puffer fish, and tasty *"capitan"* or Nile Perch, sometimes more than six foot long. One time while in a Bozo fishing village, they gave us a huge catfish that had been smoked, which was delicious! They had smoked the fish by burning dry donkey and camel manure. One time we were even given a baby ostrich! We often would see ostrich that would be tame and come right into the markets. They would be attracted to shiny or bright objects and were known to peck at people's eyes. We would see family groups, but today none are left in this region, as they were hunted to extinction. Likewise, when we first went to Mali, we would see many gazelle, but now they are extremely rare, because of population increases and hunting pressures.

Another part of our ministry was the distribution of gospel tracts and booklets to those who could read. Many children were sent to Timbuktu to the Koranic schools conducted by the marabous or Muslim teachers. These teachers housed and fed these children. After class each day, the children would each have a calabash and walk through the alleyways going from house to house calling out, *"Allah gardibou"* or "God's beggars." People would respond by putting a handful of uncooked rice or millet into their calabash. After receiving enough, it would be taken back to their teacher, who would have it cooked by a servant (really slave) girl. Their reading, writing, and memorization were all in the Arabic language. They would write on a tablet of wood on both sides using pen and ink. The pen was also made of wood or a stick. When their tablets were full, they would be washed clean with water. The water with the ink in it was then drunk by the student, who believed he was internalizing the Koran.

These students would also find scraps of paper and write verses from the Koran and fold them and sew them in leather pouches, which they sold in the marketplaces where they became good luck charms and were worn around the arm as a bracelet, or the neck as a necklace, over the lintel of the house or room and on their horses or camels, etc. While many of these students could read and write and had memorized long passages from the Koran, most did not understand the Arabic language. If you ask them to translate passages from the Koran into their language (Songhai), their response would simply be, "I don't know, but God does." In Islam, it is forbidden to translate or use any translation other than Arabic, as it is believed to be God's language, and as with any language, there is a loss of meaning in translations. We always carried gospel literature in both Arabic and French in hopes that those who could read would read and explain their reading to others.

Some large villages also had a weekly market day. We would try to be at the markets on market day where we put up a folding table with Christian literature.

Another fun thing about taking the Niger Gospel Boat to villages along the river is that because the big glass windshield reflected like a mirror, many children and even adults saw themselves for the first time. They would crowd around and make faces and laugh at themselves and the others. Can you imagine having never seen yourself as an adult? It was a tremendous revelation to them and entertainment for us. Many things and concepts that we take for granted were foreign to the Malians. For example, while we were on the boat, I asked a helper to push off from shore. He pushed with all his might on the railing of our boat while he was standing on the deck of our boat. He struggled and strained to no effect, of course, until I stopped him.

It was also entertaining watching freight be unloaded along the river. Gang planks never reached the shore, so people had to walk through mud and slosh through shallow water before getting to shore. Watching men carrying one hundred-kilogram (220 pounds!) bags of grain on their shoulders was amusing to people on the shore. It was an accident waiting to happen, and crowds would gather and wait anxiously for these men to slip. When they did slip and fall into the mud and water, the people howled with laughter! I am sure many of these men were hurt physically with that weight falling on them, but all of their egos were hurt being the subject of laughter.

Hippos were always a concern on the river. Hippos are responsible for more deaths in Africa than lions, elephants, snakes, or any other wildlife. One reason is that they appear deceptively docile, almost like cows, but they can be very aggressive if they feel threatened or have young present. We bumped the back of one once when I had the small boat and easily could have capsized. On other occasions, when families of hippos were present, they charged our boat, but we managed to avoid them. We knew of at least one missionary kid whose fishing boat was rammed by a hippos, and when it capsized, the hippo grabbed the boy and began thrashing him around in the water. He was seriously injured, but did survive.

A sixteen-mm film called *The Niger Nomad* captured the work and adventures of the Niger Gospel Boat and was shown at churches all around the United States for many years.

Another ministry associated with the river was our outboard engine repair school. I had one of the few outboard motors on the river until USAID gave to the Mali security forces twenty-five outboard motors. My concern was that whenever these forty-horsepower motors needed repairs they would seek me out, since I knew how to fix these engines. I decided to turn this concern into an opportunity and developed a plan to offer an outboard mechanics technical course and bring in Attino, the evangelist. USAID provided funds to bring mechanics from different regions along the river.

Nigh unto Death

In December 1959, Butch became very ill, and we noticed the symptoms he was having as the whites of his eyes turned yellow, his skin began to yellow, and his urine became very dark. Some medical missionaries from Liberia had visited Timbuktu a few weeks earlier, and we entertained them at our station. In the course of their stay, they shared with us that there had been an epidemic of hepatitis in Liberia, explaining to us the symptoms and how they had to bring in a very expensive medication to vaccinate their personnel. From their description of the disease, it appeared that our son had the telltale signs. A young French military doctor was in charge of the health of the entire region. I suggested to him that I thought Butch had hepatitis but he did not think so, but after a week, he finally confirmed our suspicion. He had no medication available, but we ordered something from a pharmacy in Mopti some four hundred kilometers away, which eventually arrived by mail via the once–a-week airmail service to Goundam. Butch was vomiting, had a high fever, and was severely dehydrated.

My brother Frank and his family arrived just before Christmas with the Niger Gospel Boat, which I was to transfer to Gao for use in January and February by the Zimmermans. Frank's wife Eleanor was expecting a baby, which was born shortly after Christmas. We had Butch sick with infectious hepatitis in one bedroom and a newborn baby in another room about ten feet away. Frank and Eleanor had their other five children with them, plus Sandy and Diane were home, so we had a full house.

The annual field conference was scheduled to begin in a few days in Niamey. Frank and I left for it, leaving Elaine with Eleanor and all the children, including Butch, who was showing signs of improvement. While en route to Niamey, I began feeling ill, and by the time we arrived in Niamey, I went immediately to bed. I would not get up again for several weeks. The next day, I was admitted to the hospital with acute infectious hepatitis, which at that time was not classified as hepatitis A, B, or C. During the next few weeks, I was unable to keep food down and was given constant intravenous saline solutions. My skin and eyes were dark yellow, and my weight went from 150 pounds to just over 100 pounds. I went into a coma, and the French doctor informed Mission Director Joe McCaba that I would not make it. Joe McCaba was there for the conference, and he began planning for my funeral. Another missionary in Niger, Dave Kepple, was a pilot and had a small Jodel two-seat French airplane. They decided that Dave would fly Frank back to Timbuktu and bring Elaine back for my funeral. Frank was not sure how to break the news to Elaine but was able to convince her that it was important that she return with Dave Kepple.

While in the coma, I felt like I was in a dream. I was floating in a cloud of milkweed fluff with angels on my way to heaven with no pain or nausea. This was a long, pleasant journey, but I do not recall actually seeing heaven. Within a day of Elaine's arrival, I came out of the coma.

Coming out of the coma caused me to do a lot of thinking about my future. I attributed my being alive to the prayers of my missionary colleagues during their conference, as well as our support team in America. But what about the future? I remember thinking if I would ever make it back to America that I would like to be a travel agent and give my commission to the missionaries who would use my services. Then in what almost seemed like an audible voice God said, "Who do you think you are? Telling Me what you are going to be or do!" That knocked out what little wind that was left in my sails. The song "I Surrender All" came to mind, and I have never consciously fought that battle again.

By now I was a bag of bones and was unshaven. I remember another missionary who I had never met came and shaved me. I later learned it was Mel Pittman, a new missionary. After five or six weeks in the hospital regaining my appetite, I was released and Elaine, and I went to Bob and Carol Richard's home. Carol knew my favorite meal was spaghetti. Arlene

Spurlock, another missionary, had made fresh cinnamon buns, and I pigged out on both so much that I landed right back in the hospital for another week. The doctor ordered me out of the tropics for three months of recuperation and treatments. When my weight got back up to 125 pounds, Elaine and I were reunited with our children, and we flew to southern France, where we stayed for two months. While there, I was injected almost daily with medications and vitamins. I kept the butcher in the market in Menton busy as his best client. He enjoyed telling customers what his meat did for me as he saw a twenty-pound difference in me in two months.

Our last month of recuperation was spent on the west side of France in a small resort town of Ronce les Bains, north of Bordeaux. Some very dear friends, Monsier and Madame Rene Roy, had arranged for us to occupy the small apartment on the back of a small French Reformed Chapel nestled among pine trees. I was able to preach each Sunday we were there. Normally services were held only during the months of July and August when tourists flooded this quaint enclave. The Roys lived there year round. Rene had served as a career soldier in the French army and was based in Timbuktu for several years. Nicolle accompanied her husband, and they both attended regularly our services. He was now retired and was in the real estate business. After a month in Ronce, we returned to Timbuktu. Since then, I have never had a problem with my liver, again the *hand of the Lord*. I believe Madame Roy was a believer, but Rene was not. Several years later on a visit, I asked him if he had trusted Christ as his Savior. His response was negative, so my next question was, "Why were you so faithful in attending church in Timbuktu?" He responded, "Because you lived what you preached."

Chapter 12.

The Bookstore Ministry

Thy word is a lamp unto my feet, and a light unto my path.
Psalms 119:105

The bookstore expanded to a rented store in the main market area right across the street from the meat market and was very visible. Two branch stores were opened in the cities of Gao and Niafunke where the Dan Zimmerman and the Carmichaels were stationed. Both of these were located on the properties where the missionaries lived. Christian literature was widely distributed through colportage, as all of us from time to time would visit some of the village markets. A number of villages had a particular day of the week when people from surrounding areas would come to buy and sell. These markets were filled with merchants selling cloth, grass mats, pottery, sandals, salt, and grain. Gospel booklets printed by the Scripture Gift Mission out of England in Arabic and French were popular. I think they were used more as wallets than for reading, but they were carried back into areas where the gospel had not been taken.

Our bookstores continued to bear fruit. One gentleman who had studied in Cairo, Egypt, for thirteen years would stop by and ask if we had anything to read in Arabic. He was teaching Arabic in the public schools in Timbuktu. I showed him an Arabic Bible, which he bought. As he read it, he'd send notes to me with questions. Then under the cover of darkness, he would come to me, and we would talk about his questions. Eventually, he became a Christian, and I had the privilege of baptizing him. But when he returned home from being baptized, he found that his wife had left him. Then at the end of the month, he learned that he would not be getting a paycheck and that the school had "lost" all of his paperwork. Instead of being greeted in the streets, the other men now spit at him. He had to leave Timbuktu and took a position in a small village, and from there I lost track of him.

Mentally ill people took all kinds of abuse. They would be teased, called names, and mocked, and people would even throw stones at them. The mentally ill people, including the aforementioned Mr. Abdoulai in Timbuktu, would often hang around our bookstore because they knew that we would be kind to them. Even though they might have been insane, they knew we had a heart for them and would not abuse them. One day, though, too many of them had gathered inside the bookstore, and I had become a bit impatient with them. I said to the entire group, "Okay, I want all of you who are crazy to leave." One of the ladies who indeed had mental problems pointed at each of the others and said, "That means you, and you, and you, and you, and you, and me!" And they all left.

Mental illness is seldom treated in West Africa, and in cities it is common to see mentally ill people walking naked in the streets or lying among the garbage. Mental illness is mostly ignored by governments and charitable organizations alike in favor of food programs or traditional medical aid. Few professional psychiatrists practice in West Africa. One estimate places eighty patients per psychiatrist in the United States, whereas in Sub-Sahara Africa six hundred thousand needy patients exist for each psychiatrist. And if psychiatric services do exist, they are not available to the poor. Our hearts went out to these individuals in Timbuktu. We enjoyed them, and they enjoyed having a refuge in and around the bookstore.

In the early 1960s, we took a survey among our four mission stations and found that nearly all of the national attendees in our churches and Bible classes were the result of our contacts through our bookstores.

Currency Crisis

Currency of Mali was known as CFA. In the early 1960s, the Mali government became socialistic, and one day, without any prior notice, the government issued a new currency and gave the people three days to exchange their CFA into the new Mali Franc. The CFA, based on the French franc, was traded all over French West Africa and backed by the Banque de France. It had value throughout the world, but the new Mali franc was worthless outside of Mali. The effect was that the Mali government inherited all the hard currency and the people were left with paper that had little value, even within the country, and then in addition, it was devaluated by 50 percent. Almost immediately most commodities were nationalized, and the government opened stores known as SOCOPAO. They were the only stores to sell rice, millet, sugar, flour, cooking oil, tea, and other staples. Small shops had to purchase from the government, who controlled the prices. To purchase anything outside of the country, people were required to have an import license, which in turn required a permit to purchase foreign currency. This had to be approved each time by the treasury department, who controlled all the CFA in the country. The result was the Mali government with all of this new cash spent millions of dollars (CFA), establishing embassies all over the world, mostly in communist countries, but also some Western countries and Arab countries.

Then they established their own government-owned airline. Great Britain provided them with three DC 3s, which were used within the country and on flights to neighboring African countries. The Russians supplied them with a fleet of AN2s and Illusian 14s and 18s. (The AN-2 was a bi-plane built for crop dusting. Flying on it was interesting, as the passengers sat with their backs to the walls facing each other with the freight, including goats and chickens in the middle by their feet.) The fuel for operating their airline as well as landing fees, servicing the planes, plus their ticket agents around the world all demanded hard cash, and it was not too long before the government went broke and ended up being backed up financially by the communist countries, which eventually enslaved them.

The next thing that happened was that the government opened up their own bookstores throughout the country known as the *Librairie Populaire*. They stocked these stores with books, magazines, and newspapers from Russia and China and communist groups in France. They did not compete very well with our stores, as their stock was all donated propaganda that did not interest many people. They did sell paper from China that was very inexpensive.

Our supplies, such as books, pens, notebooks, envelopes, typewriter ribbons, Christian literature, and Bibles, came from France, Belgium, Switzerland, England, and Lebanon. To beat the system, we opened a bank account in France and had our field funds sent to Paris from America and then made our own exchange to French francs from our dollars. Thus we were able to purchase our supplies and pay with French francs and from our bookstores pay our missionary salaries with Malian francs. In a sense, we were our own international bank.

The next problem we faced was that we received a notice from the government, as did all the other stores in Timbuktu and throughout the country, that we would have to pay a license to continue to operate.

There were three categories of fees: Importer-Wholesaler, the equivalent of $250,000, local store non-importer, the equivalent of $15,000, and a table store in the market, the equivalent of $1,000. We fell in the highest category, since all of our material was imported, and we were considered a wholesaler since we supplied the materials for Gao and Niafunke stores. We were given thirty days to comply or close. The license was called a "patent."

The Lord knew that this was our main ministry in Mali, especially since all of our work was in the north and almost entirely among Muslims. There was no way we would ever come up with a quarter million dollars, and God led me to decide to close our three stores immediately and not wait thirty days. I contacted Dan Zimmerman and Bill Carmichael and requested that they close their stores, which they did.

Within a couple days, the people in Timbuktu began to get angry at us because they could not buy any envelopes to mail their letters. There were no pens (we were the first to bring Bic pens into our region) or schoolbooks for their children. The schools no longer could get their books because the government had squandered the money, which affected the supplies for the schools. In effect, this caused a rippling within the community affecting the post office, the administration, and even the military, as they all had become dependent on the Librairie Evangelique for their supplies. The government-run Librairie Populaire had none of the supplies they needed. We had the excuse that we had no choice, that we could not comply with the government ruling. Now the Muslims were upset that the government was closing our bookstores, upon which they depended.

Word immediately spread to the capital in Bamako a thousand kilometers away to my friend Mohamed Alasane. He was from Timbuktu and was the president of the national assembly and the next in command under the president. He in turn contacted the minister of Finance, and they worked out an agreement that they would accept us under the second category, and we were notified of this. That meant that we would need to prove that we had a total of $15,000 in cash and stock, of which 50 percent had to be put into a blocked account in the bank that the government could seize if they found any infractions in our bookkeeping or unauthorized profit margins. I had always had a good relationship with Mohamed Alasane, and we thanked him for his intervention for us.

Prior to this whole episode, Mohamed Alasane, on behalf of the minister of tourism, asked if we would get some more postcards printed to be used throughout Mali to promote tourism in the country. Tourists coming into Mali were not permitted to take pictures in the country without having a permit from the "security," which normally took several days to obtain, and thus postcards were in some ways a substitute. I had just received over one hundred thousand new postcards, which had arrived from a printer in New Jersey.

We had taken the photos for the postcards ourselves and sent them to New Jersey to be printed. The law said you could not take photos of military, police, official buildings, bridges, naked people, lines of people waiting for gasoline or food, or anything else that might present Mali in a bad light or be what they considered a security threat. So tourists and the government relied on our postcards to show the world Mali.

After getting permission to operate our stores, we needed to come up with $15,000 in assets and put half of the amount in the blocked government account. The police came to verify that we had the amount needed, and they counted every postcard, all 100,000 of them, one by one. The government had put a fixed price of 30 Malian francs per card. They had cost us less than a penny a piece. With the cash and all the stock, which included not only postcards but also thousands of Bic pens, thousands of plastic notebook covers, and books, we had more than needed to satisfy the requirement. Before long, we were trading Bic pens to the government store for their paper products, which were cheaper for us than ordering it from France. Thanks to our fiend Alasane, it eventually got to a point where the central government in Bamako began to purchase office supplies from our little bookstore far away up in the middle of nowhere—Timbuktu. Only God could have orchestrated this! To God be the glory!

Later in Bamako, I visited the director of the government bookstores and shared with him that I had noticed that their bookstores throughout the country were missing the most important book in the world. He asked "What is it?" I told him the Bible, and he ordered 50 copies! Also, in the capital was a large department store with large glass display windows, but it only had Chinese soap for sale and occasionally powered milk from China called Great Wall Powdered Milk. It was terrible milk and even had rocks in it, although probably not from the Great Wall. I made a deal with the manager, who was looking to sell more than soap, to provide him with several hundred packets consisting of Bic pens of four colors, a piece of cardboard that contained a compass, a ruler, a protractor pencil sharpener, and a triangle, and all of these would have a Christian magazine *Champion* attached to them, which would remain attached when sold. *Champion* was published by Sudan Interior Mission and had a feature story about Mali.

On top of that, we were given permission to employ a Christian worker in the store to sell subscriptions to the monthly magazine and to display the material and magazine in their store window.

We started importing Russian Bibles from the States, and for three consecutive years, we sold more Russian Bibles than French Bibles. Many Russian teachers and advisors were common in the country in those days. If three Russians came into the bookstore, none of them would show any interest in the Bible, but then all three of them would return one by one and buy one secretly. They couldn't speak English and only a little French, but they seemed friendly to us Americans. We placed another Bible in the hands of a pilot from Czechoslovakia. He asked us what brought us to Timbuktu, and when we told him we were missionaries he couldn't believe it. It was mind-boggling to him that somebody would choose to live in Timbuktu. Foreigners were only in Timbuktu because they had been assigned or forced to go there. This really impressed him! We told him it was not a problem living in Timbuktu but a privilege to be doing God's work and sharing the good news in this needy place. We explained that although it was a difficult place to live, we had peace in our hearts knowing that this is where God wanted us to serve Him. He then shared how back in his apartment building in Prague, there was an old lady crippled with arthritis who was a Christian. Everybody knew she was a Christian and was impressed by how she was happy and never complained about her physical condition. He gladly accepted a Bible from us on his next flight into Timbuktu.

Mali's Socialistic government ran the economy into the ground, and food and services became scarce. People were starving, and there was widespread suffering. Finally there was a coup d' etat. They put the President Modibo Keita in a cage and paraded him through Bamako. They also arrested our friend, the president of the national assembly who had been so helpful to us on many occasions. They put him in a military prison in the Sahara Desert. Years later he was released, and I visited with him when he returned to Timbuktu. Although he was a Muslim, he always graciously accepted Scripture calendars I would give him. I would give him a wall calendar and also a day-by-day calendar with a small devotional on the back of each day. I believe he read those devotionals.

Chapter 13.

Our Children's Education

The fear of the Lord is the beginning of knowledge: but fools despise wisdom and instruction. Proverbs 1:7

One of the most challenging difficulties on the mission field was dealing with our children's education. Initially there only were two options, either home school or send our children to the local school up the road from where we lived. Later there would be the third option of sending them off to boarding schools. We enrolled Butch in the local school, which was taught in French. This was not a problem for him, as he had already picked up three languages by the time he was six years old, English, Songhai, and French. French was also a new language for the locals, as they all spoke Songhai. The French had a policy that the teachers they employed were from other areas of West Africa with a different native language, and thus they were forced to use French. With the teachers unable to communicate in the local language, the students quickly learned French. Butch had finished first grade in the United States while we were on furlough.

One day during our second term, I asked Butch's schoolteacher how he was doing and his reply was that he hadn't seen him in three months! It turned out he was playing hooky and spending his day with an African boy named Alasane. He lived around the corner from us in a small grass mat hut. He had learned that when the school bell (which was an old tire rim hung from the branch of a tree) rang at 7:30 AM it was time to go to school, and when it rang at noon, it was time to go home for lunch and a siesta. It rang again at 3:00 PM, which was the time for classes to start, and it rang again at 5:00 PM for the time to go home. So he would leave for school and then come home for lunch. We learned that when he was supposed to be in school, he was at Alasane's house playing. As a kid I had played hooky a few times, but not until I was in high school. The founder of our mission used to remind me, "The apple doesn't fall far from the tree!" But overall Butch had a good time and made many friends in that public school. I benefited from his friendships many times over the years as many of his playmates went on to become government officials in Bamako. I could do business in Bamako in a fraction of the time as others because of all of this relationship that I could call upon to expedite things. I was known in Bamako as "Butchie Baba" (meaning Butchie's father).

Sandy also went to the local school for a short time. Eventually we enrolled them both in the Calvert School, a correspondence home school program out of Baltimore, Maryland. This was long before home schooling became popular, and Christian curricula were not available.

As the children got older, it became more than Elaine could handle. The one-room classroom served as a bedroom. From 1:00 to 3:00 PM was siesta time when that bedroom/classroom was 101 to 105 degrees with no electricity for fans. Mailing tests and assignments back to the United States to be graded in a timely manner was not feasible in those days, so that limited correspondence course options.

To be a teacher, particularly since training and materials were not available, required enormous amounts of time and energy. Elaine also had to spend many hours each week preparing for children's Bible classes in Songhai as well as making meals and dealing with the other household responsibilities. While Elaine was doing all of this, I was busy in the marketplace at our Christian bookstore. The pressure was getting to Elaine, and when our next furlough was due, Elaine had made up her mind that she would not return to Africa unless God provided someone to teach our kids. She felt guilty about spending so much time caring for the family as compared with the time she was giving to ministry. During that next furlough, after about six months, God began working in her heart until she surrendered and she told the Lord she was ready to go back to Africa. Within a couple of weeks, we received word that the C&MA missionary school in Guinea had room for David at their boarding school. That same year our mission started a school in Niger, where Sandy and Diane could attend.

God was faithful and answered our prayer, but not until we first surrendered the education of our children to Him. But it would not be easy for us or them. David would be going into eighth grade, and he had to be at school about a month before we would be back in Africa. The Lord provided Andy and Norma Gardner, who were returning to the MK school in Mamou, Guinea, who offered to take Butch with them. Andy and Norma would be Dave's houseparents for the next three years. Sandy, Diane, Elaine, and I would leave about a month later on a cargo ship from New York to Dakar then on to Bamako and Timbuktu. It would be nearly two months before we would hear from Butch.

When we arrived in Timbuktu, the first thing we did was get our mail and look for letters from Butch. Our concern was how he would adjust, would he be happy? Did he adjust? As we opened his letters, we read them together, "Dear Mom and Dad, I am fine and this school beats the Calvert Course." He went on to share all the things he was doing. He was happy, and as we read, we both had tears running like fountains down our cheeks, forcing us to stop and dry the tears in order to read the next sentence. We were filled with joy, as God had answered our prayers once again.

Our next big challenge would be sending our girls off in an entirely different direction to Niger. They attended the new mission school in Niamey for one year. Their experience was not as positive as Butch's. Thankfully, the following year space was available for both girls at Mamou, Guinea. This enabled us to have all our kids in the same school, which was a much better situation for many obvious reasons.

The disadvantage was the distance and isolation, as Mamou was about fifteen hundred kilometers away, with virtually no road the first five hundred kilometers, so we would see our children only twice a year. However, our children would have friends and cousins there, as by this time Frank and Eleanor's children also started school at Mamou and Bill and Lois Carmichael also sent their children to Mamou.

The children had a long Christmas vacation of nearly three months and a short two-week vacation in July, which was their break in the school year. The two-week vacation did not allow our children time to come home, as it could take a week to travel one way, so Elaine and I took our vacation at that time and picked up the kids at school and took them to the coast, usually Freetown in Sierra Leone, where years before while in the navy I had written Elaine's name in the sands of that same wonderful beach.

During their longer Christmas break, we would bring them home to Timbuktu.

The trips taking the kids to and from school at Mamou provided some of the most vivid memories for us and our children. The trip was one of contrasts; lush rainforests, mountains, refreshing waterfalls, and colorful birds, butterflies, and wildflowers in Guinea, and flat, parched land devoid of vegetation and wildlife in Mali. The trip between Guinea and northern Mali was always an adventure. Memories of these trips range from sleeping on the floor of a guest house with scores of cockroaches scurrying around and over us as we tried in vain to sleep, to the children splashing in cool streams while the adults cut limbs to replace a washed-out bridge. We would pass packs of baboons and even see chimpanzees, which are now very rare in West Africa. Monkeys would be practically dripping from the trees. On a particularly memorable trip, I was driving along and the Lord caused me to glance down at the gas gauge. The needle was dropping before my eyes! I quickly stopped and found that the drain plug in the gas tank had been punched up into the inside of the tank, apparently by hitting a rock. Butch jammed a stick into the hole to stop the fuel from completely draining out on the ground. There was no AAA to call or corner gas station to walk to, but as always, God provided. I knew I would not have enough fuel to make it to Mamou. We limped into the next village. A peace corps volunteer in the village said she would ask the commandant if he would give us some fuel. She did, but the commandant refused to help us. The woman then offered us twenty liters of her gas, and I promised that we would replace it on the return trip. Off we went up into the mountains. It soon became clear that something was wrong. The car chugged and could barely make it up the mountain. I had to keep it in low gear to prevent it from stalling. It then occurred to me what happened. She had mistakenly given us kerosene instead of gasoline! I stopped and diluted the kerosene in the tank with my last 20 liters of gasoline that I had been carrying in a jerry can. That solved *our* problem, but I prayed that she would realize her mistake and not try to light her kerosene refrigerator with gasoline and blow herself up. Thankfully, she lived to get her kerosene replaced.

Between these two vacation periods, we were separated from our children for many long months at a time, which was difficult for us and them. Without modern e-mail, let alone telephone service, we would not even get to speak to them through these long periods of separation. This lack of communication was the hardest part. We never knew how they were doing in school or much else about their welfare. The school children were required to write their parents once a week, but the letters were screened for anything that might upset the parent missionaries and disrupt their ministry. Moreover, the postal system was poor and unreliable, especially after Independence, when it became even more difficult to move mail across borders of what now were different countries. We might occasionally get a letter from somebody at the school saying our child was sick, but the letter would be two weeks old by the time we got it and so we had no idea if they had gotten better or worse since the letter was sent. One time we got word that the children had played with a dog that had rabies, so all of the children at the school had to go through a whole series of rabies shots. At that time they were given thirty shots in the stomach. As you can imagine, when missionaries left their children at these boarding schools, it was a traumatic and emotional parting for the children and also the parents. But the norm and conviction of most missionaries in that era was that their calling and service to God was top priority and faith that God would take care of and meet the needs of the children.

The school at Mamou only went through tenth grade, and there were no other schools available for Butch after completing tenth grade, so he would have to leave the field. We sent him to Houghton Academy in New York State for eleventh grade. He stayed with my father in upstate New York during the holidays, and we returned to be with him on furlough for his senior year. While Dave completed his senior year in Atlantic City, New Jersey, Diane and Sandy also went to school, with Diane completing eighth and ninth grade and Sandy completing ninth and tenth grade.

In the meantime, all the former French colonies in West Africa had gained their independence in 1960. Guinea voted to sever all ties with France, and it became pretty much a police state and completely socialistic. Eventually missionary activity was repressed in Guinea, closing station after station, and the school in Mamou had to close.

In Niger, EBM's school planned to go through twelfth grade, but using correspondence courses from the University of Nebraska, supplemented by teachers to supervise the students. Diane completed tenth grade in Niger and Sandy completed twelfth grade, although she still had several correspondence courses to complete after returning home. She ultimately got her high school diploma from the University of Nebraska.

Diane was given the choice of completing high school in Niger like her sister or going back to the States for her last two years. Elaine's brother and sister-in-law Wilbur and Lorraine Beswick had offered to keep her for those two years. Diane hardly knew her uncle and aunt, but she elected to go and live with them rather than return to Niger. She wanted to be a nurse and knew that the best way to get into nursing school would be to graduate from an American high school. Wilbur Beswick was pastoring the First Baptist Church in Lansing, Illinois.

In the meantime, missions were at risk of losing missionaries, as there was nothing suitable for the education of their children on the field through high school. The struggle to carry out an effective ministry while carrying out important parental responsibilities was ripe with controversy and complications in this era in West Africa. Although some boarding schools have become rather infamous in recent years, thankfully, today the boarding schools have trained professional teachers, counselors, and dorm parents and with more frequent vacation breaks, better communications, and easier travel. So children are not as isolated from their parents as they were in times past and they have a more nurturing and positive experience while in school.

During this time, the Conservative Baptist Foreign Mission Society built a school for missionary children near Bouake in the Ivory Coast (now called Cote d'Ivoire). It also only went to tenth grade. The Conservative Baptist would not add two more years to their program unless they were assured that there would be adequate students for a full-fledged high school. Our mission, now called Evangelical Baptist Missions (EBM), was not satisfied with the supervised correspondence program in Niger. So they, along with Baptist Mid Missions, assured the Conservative Baptists that we would provide enough students for them to add eleventh and twelfth grade. Moreover we would build a dormitory to house twenty-eight students. I was assigned to draw up plans for the dorm.

We still had one more daughter to get through high school. I took Diane back to the States alone, while Elaine stayed in Timbuktu. I would be gone about a month.

Our first stop was at Dave Jr.'s home just outside of Atlantic City, New Jersey. While at Dave's, I drew up plans for the dorm. I also visited Lou Baron, who owned a print shop in Atlantic City. His establishment had had a face lift since I had done business with him in earlier years, I remarked to him, "Lou, it looks like you are making money," and he replied, "I am," and with that, he handed me a stack of $3 bills. His picture was printed on the front with him wearing a wig. On the back was a picture of his shop, which resembled a national monument. They looked real, so real that the IRS confiscated his plates and forbid him to print any more. Apparently too many people tried to pass them off to foreigners in the casinos. I showed him a $20 gold piece that I had purchased from a merchant in Timbuktu for $18 worth of Mali currency. He immediately offered me $50 for it, as he wanted to buy it for a friend because the date on it was the year of his friend's birth date. I sold it thinking it was a good deal. Little did I know that within a few months the price of gold would jump from a standard price of $35 per ounce to over $300. It turned out that I was both a winner and a loser. I had gained $32, but considering the soaring price of gold, I was a loser. I guess most people who visit Atlantic City end up losers!

Diane and I flew to Chicago from Dave's, where we were met by my brother-in-law, Wilbur. After exchanging greetings, I gave him my black bag, which had inscribed in gold printing, "Air Mali." In the bag were our passports, my return ticket to Mali and Timbuktu, all of my money, the deed to our property and mobile home in New Jersey, and a pile of those $3 bills. I gave my bag to Wilbur and suggested that he get the car while we retrieved our luggage. We had about an hour drive to Lansing, Illinois. On arrival in Lansing, we unloaded our baggage, and I said to Wilbur, "I don't remember seeing my black bag." We began to search and it was nowhere to be found. We immediately called O'Hare airport to see if perhaps someone found it and turned it in. We learned every airline had its own "lost and found." We assumed that Wilbur laid my bag on the hood of the car next to his while he unlocked his car and forgot to pick it up before driving out. The person we talked to on the phone gave us the phone number of the toll gate where we had exited. No one had turned it in, but the gentlemen offered to go look for it when he was not busy. We drove back, but three hours had gone by. We looked where the car had been parked and found nothing. I remember silently praying, asking the Lord to help us. Next we went into the terminal asking each airline if anyone turned in a black bag. We were told that the city had a "lost and found" in the police station upstairs.

Going up the steps, we passed a policeman who was coming down, so I asked him where I could find the "lost and found." His response was, "Are you looking for a black bag?" When we arrived at the door, we found two police officers with the black bag on a table, and they had a sheet of paper writing down an inventory of everything in the black bag. They were in the process of counting three-dollar bills. I didn't know if I should admit that the black bag was mine for fear of having what looked like counterfeit money. They did not say a word about the $3 bills, and they put everything back in the bag and handed it to me. I thanked them and the Lord. It was now midnight, and the black bag had been lost for four hours in Chicago where someone, a very honest person, found it and gave it to an honest policeman, who in turn gave it to the officers on duty at the station, who were also honest, and I was once again in possession of over $300 in cash, my passports, my tickets from Chicago to Timbuktu, my worthless $3 bills, and many valuable papers. Do I believe in guardian angels? Yes! One was on duty at the O'Hare airport in Chicago.

My next challenge was hugging Diane and saying good-bye to our baby girl, who we would not see for two years until we attended her high school graduation. This too was a very difficult time for us, as again we were separated from our children.

Providing a Place for Other Children

The plans that I had drawn up were submitted to the government for a permit to begin construction. They were inspected and were approved within about two days, another miracle. On January 1, 1971, Elaine, Sandy, and I moved to Bouake to begin the dorm construction, which included fourteen bedrooms for students, an infirmary to house sick students, another large room for nurses' quarters with a bath for both the nurse and one for the infirmary, plus two large bathrooms at each end of the building. There was also a room for visitors and an apartment for the house parents.

Elaine and I took four men from Mali to help with the construction. These men mixed by hand all the concrete for the footings, reinforced pillars, floors, and second floor. They worked extremely hard, and we compensated them well. Once when I returned to Timbuktu during the construction period, I was working in my office when a very large Tuareg appeared at the door dressed in all his regalia with his face veiled, spear in his hand, sword on his side, and a dagger on his arm, plus fetishes hanging from his turban and anywhere he could put them. I could see he was upset. He began to accuse me of stealing his slave. Within a couple of minutes, I realized he was referring to Dick, one of the men I had taken to Ivory Coast. Dick was a nickname that we had given to our strongest laborer. He reminded us of Dick DeWees, who had invited me to Vacation Bible School years before. I assured this massive Tuareg nomadic tribesman that I was not aware that Dick was a slave and that he belonged to a master. I explained that he had often worked for me, and because he was a good worker, I invited him to accompany me for a construction job in the Ivory Coast. After about a half hour and the assurance that I would return his slave to him after the job was completed, he was satisfied. I regret that I missed the opportunity to share with him how that I was once a slave to sin but Christ paid a great price to set me free.

During the eight months that we spent building the dorm, often other missionaries from Liberia and Ghana came to give a helping hand, so Elaine was the hostess and cook. Once a week we would relieve the dorm parents of GMU for the afternoon and evening to give them a break. It was always a time of great fellowship.

Chapter 14.

Serving By Leading

But God has chosen the foolish things of the world to confound the wise; and God hath chosen the weak things of the world to confound the things which are mighty. 1 Corinthians 1:27

In 1972, we returned to the United States on our furlough and also to attend Diane's high school graduation. Prior to leaving Mali, the home office asked that I meet with the board for an interview, as Rev. Joseph McCaba had suggested me as a candidate for the position of general director of the Mission. The Mission had been without a director for two years. During this period, the number of missionaries declined from about ninety to fifty-five. The board was made up of godly men living in North New Jersey and Long Island, New York. They met monthly starting at 5:00 PM or later and began with the reading of the minutes and the treasurer's report. Then they would break for dinner and go to a local restaurant and reconvene about 8:00 PM. As missionaries, we always received a copy of their minutes. It was not unusual to read that the meeting adjourned around midnight and sometimes as late as 1:00 AM. Some of the most important decisions were being made after midnight.

During my interview, they asked what direction I would take the mission if I were the director. I immediately responded that business would not be conducted after ten o'clock in the evening. Second, I would trust the Lord to get the "general fund" out of the red within a couple of months, and third, we would enlarge the board with members from other geographical areas, especially from the Midwest, the source of most of our missionaries and support. I offered to try to conserve my support base and not draw any salary from the general fund until we were out of debt. The board did not accept my proposal but rather that I would be paid a salary from the general fund and that all of our personal support would go into the general fund. I was appointed general director effective September 1972.

Our staff was Mrs. Rose Kassack, a very efficient secretary whom I credit with holding the mission together during the two years we were without a director. Rose spoke French fluently, the language most of our missionaries used in both ministry and dealing with foreign governments. We had a part-time bookkeeper who also did all the receipting. I was the third person in the office, but my responsibilities often took me away for days and sometimes weeks at missionary conferences all over the country in churches and Bible colleges. We were living at the Houses of Fellowship in Ventnor, New Jersey. When I was not at conferences, I had a foam mattress that I laid in front of my desk where I slept at night. I drove home to Ventnor for the weekends. Within two months, the general fund was back in the black after being in the red for over a year.

Our office was three rooms that we rented in a commercial complex. Previously our office had been on Broadway in Patterson, New Jersey. But Patterson became plagued by crime. Several times our office was broken into and office equipment stolen. Homeless people lived in it at night, and the insurance rates kept going up. Therefore, the board sold the property and had $35,000 to use for a new building. We began looking for property away from New York City. In the early years, New York City was a convenient location since most missionaries traveled on cargo ships, which had no exact time schedules. Their business was freight, not passengers, thus it was convenient to have guest rooms along with office space near the port. But property near New York City became too expensive, so we looked at a large garage that was for sale in South Jersey. It was a shell that could have been divided into offices. However, during my first month as director, I had meetings at Bible Baptist Church in Kokomo, Indiana, and I shared with Pastor Ben Strohbehn that we were looking for a place to relocate our offices. He said "Why not Kokomo?" I said, "Wherever the Lord leads." The church took on the challenge and began to pray. A couple months later, we received a call advising us of a building for sale along highway 31, the main route between Indianapolis and South Bend. A board member, Rev. Richard Pettitt was planning a trip to Indianapolis, so we asked him to look at the property and bring us pictures and a report. This building was built as a duplex home but was being used as a mortuary. The pictures showed a room full of caskets and another small room where bodies were washed. I joked with Dick, asking him if he heard any of the caskets talking to each other. He said. "No, why?" I said, "I thought you would hear one of them asking, 'Is that you coughin'?'"

Five of us flew to Indiana to view the property, and at the next board meeting, the board voted unanimously to make an offer of $55,000 for it. The next day, I called the realtor and made the offer. The following day, they accepted the offer. Little did we know that a lady none of us knew had died almost a year before and had left $20,000 to the mission. The check came in the mail the very same day that we closed on the property. So with the $35,000 that we had on hand from the sale of the Paterson property plus the $20,000 from the estate of the deceased lady, we had the exact amount to the penny for the purchase of the property. Only God could have arranged this and given us assurance that the decision that was made was of the Lord!

We were on our way to Kokomo exactly one year to the day that I had begun my duties as general director. We arrived on Saturday night of the Labor Day weekend, September 1973. With Labor Day being a holiday, Bible Baptist Church arranged for a good group of members to welcome us and help us with the unloading of our U-Haul at our new headquarters.

The board had already provided that the north end of the duplex would be used as housing for Elaine and me. It had three small bedrooms and one bath, a kitchen, and a small living room. The south side of the building would be used for the office.

By Tuesday morning, we were operational. The Lord had provided personnel. Bob Manning, a retired marine, was our accountant. He had come to New Jersey for a week to acquaint himself with our accounting system and the general office procedures. He was on "deck" at 8:00 AM on Tuesday morning as well as Connie Johnson, a secretary and a member of the Bible Baptist Church. Thus we made the move to Kokomo, Indiana, without missing a day of work. By Tuesday, we were receipting support for the missionaries, had opened a bank account, changed our mailing address, and hired our new staff—Connie and Bob.

As the Mission grew, we added additional staff, a bookkeeper, Janet Agal, and a deputation secretary, Dick Pettitt, who had served as a board member for several years. Dick and his wife, Dot, moved into a trailer court across the highway from our office. Dot served as Dick's secretary and also helped with posting in the finance office. She was a volunteer. My father, James Marshall, was a volunteer in the mailing department. Elaine too volunteered, creating the "Prayer Letter Service"—a service to missionaries in maintaining their mailing lists, typing their letters, getting them printed, addressing envelopes, inserting the letters into the envelopes, sorting them in zip code order, bundling them, and delivering them to the post office. She was assisted by a host of faithful volunteers from Bible Baptist Church. The Lord provided volunteers who loved to serve the Lord and saved the mission thousands of dollars.

Our move to the Midwest opened many new opportunities to the mission. EBM was an approved agency of the General Association of Regular Baptist Churches (GARBC), and the majority of these churches were located in the Midwest. Thus we had greater exposure to these churches.

Shortly before moving to Kokomo, we had our first candidate school. We held it at the Sacandaga Bible Conference grounds in Broadalbin, New York, in July 1973. Our class was small and included only six new candidates but that was 600 percent more than the previous year. It included David and Carol Richards for Mali, Steve and Julia Nunemaker for Niger, and Oliver and Grayce Kautzer for Sweden. God was so good to us in providing new missionaries and new fields of service. During my twenty-one years of ministry as director, the Lord opened fields in Argentina, Benin, Ivory Coast (Cote d'Ivoire), Zambia, South Africa, Nigeria, Romania, Germany, Sweden, Italy, Japan, French Guinea, student ministries at Iowa State University in Ames, Iowa, and Purdue University in West Lafayette, Indiana, a film ministry, Harvest Productions, a printing ministry in the USA and Romania, and Arabic ministries in the United States and France.

Our office building in Kokomo had a room large enough to display six or seven coffins. We used this room as a workroom for mailings of our quarterly bulletin and our daily mailing of receipts It also was used for cleaning and inspection of four documentary films, which included, *The Niger Nomad* on the ministry in Mali, *Desert Harvest* about Niger, *Building Amid Ruins*, on Martinique, and *Yes and Good-Bye*, a dramatic film on the calling of a missionary.

While doing *Yes and Good-Bye,* a new ministry developed under the leadership of Don Ross, called Harvest Productions, a film ministry primarily to produce evangelistic films overseas in foreign languages and adapted to foreign cultures. Harvest Productions produced its first film, *Telling Kelli,* filmed in Hawaii. Many productions have since been produced in scores of different languages.

Another unique ministry that God gave to us was that of music in missions through Ed and Sharon Karakaian. Ed was a graduate of Julliard School of Music, and Sharon was a graduate of the music department of Houghton College. They served the Lord through special music and concerts in the United States, Europe, and Africa. Years later, they would teach music and English at our Double Harvest school in Haiti. Missionaries commented that their ministry in music and testimony brought people to services who otherwise would never have come.

The Lord enabled us to conduct a retreat for our MKs (missionary kids). Many of these young people were in college or separated by thousands of miles from parents, and so holiday periods could be especially difficult for them. The retreat was held for several days between Christmas and New Years. Each MK was encouraged to bring a friend. Bible Baptist Church had a nearby lodge in a beautiful setting. Joe Stowell was our featured speaker. Lodging and meals were donated. Elaine and I often had opportunity to visit and entertain our MKs on college campuses. Many of these young people are serving the Lord on mission fields today.

Elaine and I saved money and purchased a lot southwest of Kokomo and eventually built our own house. We moved into our new home just prior to Christmas 1976. My Dad, who was living with us, had passed away and was with the Lord just a couple weeks prior to our move. Traveling from our home to the mission building every day, we would pass a beautiful insurance office building. As we were driving by, one day Elaine said to me almost jokingly, "Wouldn't it be nice if some day the Lord would give that building to EBM?" I'm not sure how I responded but probably I just thought, "Dream on."

A year or so later on a Saturday-morning shopping trip, we noticed many cars and people at the insurance building. We said together, "I wonder what's going on there?" At church the next day, I asked someone, "What was going on at the insurance company yesterday?"

"They were having an auction. They went bankrupt," was the reply.

Monday morning on my way to work I stopped and went in and noticed people loading desks and filing cabinets into trucks, things they had purchased on Saturday. I asked who was in charge, and I was pointed to a gentleman representing the Indiana State Insurance Bureau. I asked him what they were going to do with the building. He said eventually it would be put up for bids. I gave him my business card and told him we would be interested in knowing when it would be up for bids. Months went by, and finally we received information soliciting a bid. We submitted a bid, and again time went by without an answer. Finally we got a phone call from the insurance bureau in Indianapolis informing us that they felt our bid was too low and asked if we would consider going higher. In effect, what he was telling me was that either we were the only one who bid or we were the highest bidder, so I informed them that we would not go higher. Several weeks later, we learned that our bid for the building was accepted. We did not have to do any remodeling. It was ready for occupancy. Several men from our staff and the church came on a Saturday morning with pickups and had everything moved by noon. Phones were operational, and not one minute of our office hours were disrupted. Our office building on the highway was put up for sale immediately, but did not sell. Why? Because an omnipotent God had plans beyond what we knew or could imagine. We never borrowed a penny from the bank. Jimmy Carter was our president, and interest rates were as high as 21 percent for a thirty-day jumbo CD. We rented out the old office to pay off what we had borrowed from ourselves. We also had Harvest Productions move their operation from Warsaw, Indiana, into the old building, which gave us better operational consolidation with this growing ministry.

God was blessing the ministry in a very unique way. We had grown from about fifty-five to about two hundred missionaries. All of our bills were paid, and we were able to help many of our missionaries who were struggling financially. Funds were available to help new churches overseas with interest-free loans for construction.

Then one Thursday morning about 3:30 AM, we were awakened by the sheriff advising us that the mission office was on fire. Within minutes we were on the scene. It was obvious nothing could be saved. Fortunately, at the back of the building when the burning roof fell in, the wet insulation covered two file cabinets that had the minutes and the history of EBM from its founding in 1928. Jerry Paxson, our treasurer, had backed up the computer two days prior and had the discs at his home, and thus most of the financial records were saved. Working with the bank on recent deposits, we could reconstruct about 99 percent of all our financial data. The fire continued to burn throughout the day, and the fire department had to return a couple of times during the next days as the flames reignited, especially since much of the structure had fallen into the basement.

A television station in Indianapolis was on the scene that morning, and the national news services were covering the "tragedy." I began receiving phone calls at home before noon from people wanting to represent us to the insurance company (for a fee of course), and we declined their help, knowing that we were in "good hands"; no, not those hands—the Lord's! Why had our other building not sold? The answer was obvious. We still had a building. We did not "move" back because nothing was left to move. Everything was gone. The fire was so hot that there was not even a trace of the toilets in what were the restrooms. Ceramic envelope moisteners burned with no trace of them to be found. The large safe was still intact, but the contents were ashes. But we occupied our old building and worked from it. By the next day, Saturday, businesses, churches, and individuals came to our rescue and loaned chairs, desks, and tables. The phone line to our previous office was reconnected, and our staff was notified to report for work on Monday. Our insurance company in Fort Wayne told us to go out and purchase what was essential to operate, such as typewriters, computers, and stationary. Our insurance company was wonderful to us. Monday morning we were back to work, having lost only one day of work.

Soon I began getting phone calls from the local bank presidents inviting me to join them for lunch. These were business lunches for them. They assured me that they would provide help in financing for the reconstruction of our building. At that time any construction going on in Kokomo had a large sign visible from the street saying "Financed by First National Bank" or whatever the name of the bank was that was loaning the money for construction. EBM had already established its credibility in Kokomo and had the highest rating in the published financial ratings. We were known for paying our bills before they were due, and thus the banks were ready to do business. I thanked them for lunch and for their willingness to do business, but I told them we were going to erect a sign saying, "Paid for by God's People."

I spent much of the next month at the drawing board designing a building to fit our previous foundation. The First Baptist Church of Elkhart, Indiana, took on a "Thanksgiving Project" to add a second floor to the building. This would provide us with two efficiency apartments plus four motel-type guest rooms completely furnished. These would be used for missionary guests, retired missionaries who volunteered in the office, lodging for some board members during their meetings, and housing for candidates during the two weeks of candidate school.

I served as the general contractor. I was responsible to obtain all the building permits from the state in Indianapolis, which the architect estimated would take about three months. He was surprised that the Lord provided all the permits in less than three weeks.

We contacted Continental Baptist Missions to see if they had some builders available, and they did. I rented a mobile office on a trailer, and soon the missionary builders began to arrive with their mobile homes. We had five trailers on the lot and funneled all the sewage into the old septic tank. Volunteers from churches all over the Midwest came to help build the new mission building. Carol Barnes, who served as my secretary, was responsible for purchasing the furnishings, working along with the architectural firm. The building was completed just about one year from the date of the fire. We never lacked one cent in the process of construction, and when we had the dedication service on a Sunday afternoon, it was complete with all brand new furnishings and 100 percent paid for thanks to sister mission boards, many individuals, churches, and an insurance company that was sympathetic to our needs.

On top of this, the Lord provided an additional building at the back of the property, which we rented to the Howard Print Shop, a Christian family business. Landscaping and indoor plants were provided by Green Circle Growers and Heartland Growers. Again the *hand of the Lord* provided a brand-new facility, fully equipped with a value double of that which was lost. But more than that, we were blessed by friends who came to our rescue and worked to bring beauty from ashes.

David officiating a board meeting in Kokomo at the mission office

Fire at the mission office that destroyed 100% of the building

Praise the Lord!

Retreat for missionary kids, about a dozen returned to the foreign mission field

Romanian Christians who helped construct the print shop

Twelve thousand canning jars filled with food arrive in Romania

Romanian lady receiving jars with food

Dedication of the first three classrooms in Haiti

First kindergarten class in Haiti

Flag Day, children parade through the greenhouses

As in Africa, Haitian children "Use their head!" in carrying water to their homes

Chapter 15.

Romania

By reason of the multitude of oppressions they make the oppressed to cry; they cry out by reason of the arm of the mighty. Job 35:9

With the fall of communism in eastern Europe, Romania was now open to the gospel. Bill Carmichael, our European director, led a survey trip to Romania, along with other men from our mission. They visited Arad in the northwestern part of the country. Bill came back excited about the opportunities that were opening up to help churches that had been either closed or restricted in such a way that many had to meet in secret. Now with freedom, these churches were bursting with the opportunity to start new churches.

A second trip was planned with two prospective missionary couples, Bill and myself. On Bill's trip, he learned from Pastor Gongola in Arad that someone in Germany had given their church a printing press. Dave Howard, the owner of the Howard Print Shop, decided to join us on the trip to see the press and assess the potential for starting a printing ministry. The country was completely devoid of Christian literature. Dave was disappointed when he found that the printing press was not really a press but rather more of a mimeograph machine. While this was disappointing, God used it in His own way for good. Upon returning home to the office, almost immediately I received a phone call from two Christian businessmen in Indianapolis. I had never heard of these men. They shared with me that they would like to build a church building in South Africa and asked if I would draw up some plans and visit them in Indianapolis with the plans and a cost estimate. They specified that they wanted to build it in the city of Kokstad.

I immediately started drawing and came up with a set of plans within a couple days. I drove to Indianapolis and met with them. I explained to them that I was unable to give them a good cost estimate Their response was, "Don't worry. We'll take care of it." I told them that I wanted the church to be responsible for part of it as a matter of principle. (The church eventually took care of the furnishings for it, whereas these gentlemen paid for the rest of it as promised.) While talking with them, I mentioned that I had just returned from Romania and that our printer went with us and the disappointment in the machine the church had received. Their response was, "What do you need?" I said, "I don't know, but I'll get a list from Dave." Little did we know that they had recently acquired at auction all of the printing equipment from a large printing establishment in Pennsylvania that had gone bankrupt. The printing equipment was sitting on three floors of a warehouse not far from their office. I arranged for Dave to go down to see what could be used. As we went into the building I thought Dave's eyes would burst as he looked at presses, huge paper cutting machines, binding machines, cameras, and more. "Whatever you can use, help yourself." Now only God could have orchestrated that! But that's only the beginning!

While I was in Romania, I went into a "supermarket." I found that it was virtually empty. The only things on the shelves were glass jars filled with white beans. There were two prices. One was the deposit on the jar, and the other was the price of the beans, which was less than the deposit. Apparently you could find dry beans cheaper somewhere else.

That was it! There was nothing for sale but beans that looked like they had been there for years. I then went to a store that only sold bread. A line of people extended out the store and down the block. They would run out before the people could all be served.

Along the street, there was a sidewalk. Between the sidewalk and the street was a dirt plot about four or five feet wide. I noticed women with hoes chopping the dirt and planting vegetable seed. Behind their houses were large fields that had been confiscated from their owners by the communist government, but it would take time for the new government to go through the courts to return this property to its owners, especially since many of the former owners had died and records had been destroyed.

In the middle of the night, the Lord woke me, and all I could think of was Romanian women chopping up the hard soil along the street hoping to plant and get a small harvest to supplement their food ration. I also could see the sheep, goats, geese, chickens, and cows that roamed the street looking for something to eat. These patches of vegetable gardens would have little chance at survival. My mind drifted to the empty shelves in the supermarket. How could we help these poor people? The idea that the Lord brought to mind was to provide them with canning jars that we would fill with flour, sugar, rice, pasta, dry beans, etc. By 6:00 AM I was in our supermarket, where the shelves were always full of everything imaginable. The hardest problem we face in America is choosing which brand to buy. The first thing I bought was a case of quart canning jars, and then bags of sugar, flour, rice, and spaghetti. My cart was full. From there I went to the office, arriving a little before seven o'clock. I put everything on the table and opened all the bags and cartons and began filling the twelve canning jars, taking care to weigh the contents of each jar and keeping a record so we would know how much of the product it would take to fill a case.

Within a day or so, we had a board meeting, and I challenged our board members with the project of filling cases of canning jars with food to be sent to Romania. Most board members were pastors who in turn challenged their churches. The response was tremendous. While we had not yet received any money, by faith we ordered one thousand cases of canning jars.

We had figured how much food it would take to fill the jars. Bible Baptist Church allowed us to store the jars and food in their auditorium, which was also a gym. Two men from the church were assigned to purchase the food. Bill Carmichael coordinated everything. A tractor trailer arrived from a distribution center in Kentucky and unloaded one thousand cases of jars along a wall inside the auditorium. Along the back wall there were hundred-pound bags of rice, sugar, beans, etc. On Sunday morning, when several hundred members arrived at church and saw the display of jars and food, they were challenged during the service to come back on Monday morning at 8:00 AM to open a thousand cases, open twelve thousand quart jars, and fill each jar and then reseal the jars, put them back in the cases, then sprinkle wrapped candies to fill all the void spaces between the jars and reseal the cartons with tape. Outside, seven or eight pickup trucks were standing by. They hauled the jars to the EBM mission about a half mile away where another crew unloaded them into a forty-foot shipping container. The Channel 6 television crew from Indianapolis was on hand, and it was featured on the nightly news that evening. By 3:00 PM everything was ready for shipment to Romania, along with two other forty-foot containers filled with cases of baby food, orange juice, and tons of other supplies. The Lord accomplished all of this through His people. It was a wonderful day seeing the excitement of about seventy-five people working together to serve people thousands of miles away. It was my privilege to be in Romania when it arrived and be involved in the distribution through the Baptist churches in Romania.

I was joined in Romania by a group of Christian businessmen, the VanWingerdens, Jim Gapinski, and Ron Pierre. These men owned greenhouses in seven or eight states and are heavily involved in mission projects. I didn't realize then that they would become such important people in the course of my life. These men provided farm equipment for a cooperative run out of the Baptist church in Alexandria, Romania. They provided several tractors, along with implements, a combine, wagons, two large silos, and a flour mill.

We traveled together to Alexandria and to Zimmencia. In our hotel in Alexandria, the hallways had no lights, so we had to light matches to find our rooms. There was no hot water, and the beds were cot size. The light in the room was at best about twenty-five watts. The Baptist church in Alexandria had a small branch church in the town of Zimmencia along the Danube River. They were meeting in a small room on the first floor of a communal apartment building and needed a building of their own. Again we saw the Lord provide a vacant lot and the material to construct a nice building. A Presbyterian church in Indianapolis provided materials as well as a work team. Our good friends Ted and Jenell Lozier were on site and responsible for the construction. No Presbyterian churches existed in Romania, but Presbyterian churches in the United States with a heart for missions took responsibility for building several Baptist churches.

I left my friends in Bucharest where they were to fly to Amsterdam. They discovered upon take-off that they were flying east instead of west. They were on a Romanian airline, and apparently there was no aviation fuel in the capital city, thus they were flying to another city in Romania that had fuel to fill up in order to make it to Amsterdam.

I returned to Arad, where we wanted to develop a printing ministry. I had rented a car and was praying I'd find a gas station that had gas. While filling my tank, I noticed another man filling his tank on the opposite side of the island, and he did not look like a Romanian, so I spoke to him, and lo and behold, he was a medical doctor from Indianapolis. We had spoken to each other by phone about ten days earlier back in the States! He had called, me having heard of our ministry in Romania. He was heading east to Bucharest, and I was going west. We had talked to each other thousands of miles away in Indiana but had never met, but here at a gas station we met for the first time. How can such a thing happen? Again the *hand of the Lord!*

Upon my arrival back in Arad, I found that John and Mike, the men who provided the funds for the church building in Kokstad, South Africa, and who had provided the printing equipment for us, were still in Arad. Together we went to look at a piece of property that would be suitable for starting the print shop. The property was located on a dead-end street with a school at the end. It had a one-story house with four rooms. The yard was big enough to accommodate a building about thirty-five feet by twenty-five feet. The asking price was $10,000. John and Mike provided the money, and we purchased it through the Baptist church. Previously under the oppressive communist government, it was illegal to own or operate a printing press in Romania. The dollar was at a very high value against the Romanian currency. Now was the time to advance our ministries, as the government was in disarray and no one knew who was in charge. The next challenge was to train somebody to operate the print shop. Two men stood out at the Baptist Church, Trian and Mercha. They both had jobs. By faith, they would have to give up their work. We decided to bring them to the States to work at the Howard Print Shop for a period of three months. This meant leaving their families in Romania. Both were married men with children. They were fairly fluent in English, and they adjusted well. I can still remember seeing the tears running down their cheeks the first time they were taken to a supermarket. They could not believe we had so much and so many varieties and brands. We housed them in the apartment at the mission. They were good students and learned well. Typesetting on the computer was both challenging and fun for them. Dave Howard's son Bruce was capable in every area of the printing business. It was not long before Bruce and his wife Brenda volunteered to go along with their young daughter to Romania for two years to help set up and train the men there on site.

It became apparent that we needed an additional building in Romania to house the printing equipment and make it operational. So, I designed a building to fit on the back of the property. Heartland Growers in Indiana had a large warehouse about twenty miles from Kokomo. Jim Gapinski was gracious and allowed me to prefab a twenty-five-by-thirty-five-foot building there in his building. I built the complete shell, installing doors and windows.

While I was building this, I received a phone call from a medical doctor. He had heard that we were involved in Romania and told me he had been given several tons of space on a U.S. air force C5 cargo plane going to Bucharest. I explained that I had a whole building that I'd like to ship, but he said everything must fit on pallets. I told him I would get back to him within a couple hours. I called my brother Don, who worked as an estimator for a very large construction company in Philadelphia. I wanted to see if he could take a day off and make a lot of purchases for me and get it delivered to a warehouse in Lancaster, by 5:00 PM on Thursday. This was Wednesday afternoon. My brother said he'd call me back in the morning and let me know. That evening in prayer meeting, I shared a prayer request that the Lord had provided free cargo space on the largest U.S. air force cargo plane that was going to Romania, but I had to get the materials purchased and delivered by 5:00 PM the next day.

On Thursday morning, I called my brother back, and he told me that it would be impossible for him to take off work, but that he had a friend in Lancaster who was a building contractor he had worked with plus, he owned a hardware and lumber company in Lancaster and that he would be willing to help me. "The man is a Christian, but he will not be available until 1:00 PM." He gave me his name and phone number and the name of the company. That was not going to give me much time, but it was the best I could do—excuse me, it was the "best God could do." It was much better than I could do, or anyone else. At one o'clock I called and explained that I was about to give him an order on the condition that in less than four hours it needed to be delivered to a warehouse that belonged to a Dr. Niemeyer. The gentleman responded, "I know exactly where it is, as I tried to buy the same warehouse. Dr. Niemeyer and I are friends, and we both serve on the board of Lancaster Bible College!"

So my brother Don had no truck, probably no money to shop for me, but God put together His team, none of which I had ever met, and at 5:00 PM on Thursday, they delivered all the rolls of felt tar paper, shingles to cover the roof, a toilet, a vanity, gallons of paint, nails, buckets of drywall compound, screws, plus three tons of rice, flour, sugar, etc. This was all shrink wrapped and put on to pallets and then trucked to Andrews Air Force Base, where it was loaded onto that huge plane. Dr. Niemeyer had given the name of a gentleman who worked at the Pentagon along with his phone number in case we needed to contact him or ran into any problems in Romania. This gentleman would be going to Romania on this cargo plane. My next problem was to get in touch with Trian and Merchia in

Romania and have them get to Bucharest to receive the materials. It all worked like clockwork. They could not believe how big a C5 cargo plane was! It dwarfs a 747 plane. There were no problems only miracles.

As far as the building that I pre-fabbed at the Heartland Growers facility, we packed it, along with all the drywall four-by-twelve-foot sheets for the walls and ceiling. In addition, we had silos, augers, a grist mill, and other material packed into the "high cube" shipping container. It was overweight, but there were no scales between our location and the rail yard.

The Baptist church in Grundy Center, Iowa, put together a work team of about ten men to go to Romania to assemble the print shop building. We met in Chicago and were scheduled on the Romanian airlines. Our plane had arrived, but for some reason, it was delayed, and we were put into the airport hotel for several hours. I think they had to arrange for credit to buy fuel!

A couple of people from the Baptist Church in Arad met us when we landed in Timisoara, about fifty miles from Arad. It was Saturday afternoon. We learned that the container, which had been shipped over a month earlier had not yet arrived. Then we learned that the concrete slab the Romanian church was to have poured was not complete and only two-thirds of it had been poured. Here we were ten men who had taken their vacation time to come, and now they might have nothing to do. Sunday morning our spirits were raised by seeing the church full and running over with people standing outside in the cold looking in the windows. The music was exceptional, so this was a big boost. Now it was God's turn again for another miracle. Early Monday morning, we went to the building site. We were joined by about eight Romanian Christians. Trian had already ordered concrete, and we were waiting for its arrival. I had been given the phone number of a contact in Austria who was responsible for the transport of our container. It was a miracle that we were able to get a phone installed at the house of the print shop. Normally people could wait a couple years for a phone under the communist regime, and very few phones were available. It would be another miracle to make an international phone call, but at least I could try. It was 8:00 AM, and I placed my call and within minutes there was an answer in Vienna. I asked for the man whose name had been given me. "I'm sorry, he is not in yet, call back in an hour," the lady said. Okay, I'll call back.

Our container had been off loaded in Hamburg, Germany, and would come by truck all the way through Germany, Austria, Hungary, and finally into Romania. After my first attempt to locate the gentleman in Austria, the concrete truck arrived with its load. I went into the house to get my camera, as I wanted to take a picture of them unloading this miniature (compared to American size) concrete truck. Whoops! I was too late; the driver had dumped it all in the middle of the road, and all I saw was the truck speeding down the road in the distance. Our Romanian workers came with their wheelbarrows and shovels and began wheeling it to the partially finished floor. I returned to the phone, and within minutes, God gave another miracle. I had my man. He assured me that the container should arrive "today." I thanked him and hung up the phone, thinking that's like "the check is in the mail" but "Oh ye of little faith," at exactly noon, we got word that our container was at the border. Mercha and Trian were dispatched to go locate it and begin the custom formalities.

Twelve hours later at midnight, they returned, informing us that all the paperwork was complete, and at 7:00 AM, the tractor trailer with the forty-foot container was backing up the street. Our Grundy Center team and Romanian crew began immediately to unload. The concrete slab and the floor had "set up" over night. We blocked the street with the silos and other agricultural equipment and carried the walls to their respective areas, laying them in place on the floor. By 5:00 PM, all the walls were set up, and a few trusses were in place supporting the walls. Our truck driver informed us that he was fined for being over weight, but apparently the shipping company picked up the tab. He had a brand-new step ladder tied on top of our container that he purchased in Germany, and I was able to buy it from him. We did not have a ladder on the job, and it seemed like the Lord knew we needed one, so He sent it along. It served getting up and down into the container as well as on the construction site. Our truck driver was from Turkey and a Muslim. I shared with him that the building he brought to us was to be used to house a print shop that would print Christian literature. His response was jokingly that had he known what he was delivering that he would not have brought it. We thanked our driver and thanked him for selling us his new ladder and watched him haul away the container that we had overloaded in Indiana. The container was immediately replaced by another large truck that we had negotiated with a driver to take the remainder of the farm equipment, including the silos, to the area of Alexandria several hundred miles away.

By the next day, after a good night's sleep, all the trusses were in place, the sheathing covered the trusses, and the felt tar paper and some shingles were on. Once this was covered, the electrical wiring was done and dry walling was begun, followed by painting. Eight days after the container arrived, we had the dedication service. This was attended by the mayor, a Christian, as well as the building inspector, who was a woman. We had applied for a building permit but never received one. There was still the bureaucracy that prevailed. The building inspector was so fascinated with drywall that she had never seen before and with the fact that the building was constructed in less than a week that she signed the papers after the fact. Missionaries John Clayton and David Haag were present for the dedication, as they had just completed a Bible teaching series for pastors in the city of Aradia north of Arad. The men from Grundy Center did an excellent job. This entire episode was orchestrated by God, even down to the need that we had for a ladder, which we had forgotten, but God knew we needed it and caused a Turkish truck driver to purchase one for us in Germany.

Another miracle was that a paper wholesaler in Indianapolis had cases of paper they were willing to donate. We dispatched a truck to bring it to Kokomo. This was the same time we were packing and shipping the canning jars filled with food to Romania. Before loading the cases into the steel container, I thought I'd better open a case to be sure that it was worth shipping. To my amazement, the paper that had been donated was a very high-quality white. I saw that the reason that it was being disposed of was that it was cut to European or metric size, exactly what we would need in Romania. Again God had provided a good supply of paper, all cut to size. There was at least a ton of it. Thank You, Lord!

Over a period of months and with much help, we assembled the silos and farm equipment in Alexandria. Then we turned our attention to constructing the church building in Zimnecia on the Danube River. Building in the former communist country was a challenge. This was evidenced by the fact that most buildings had been built poorly and certainly unprofessionally by our standards. For example, stairways were uneven and not consistent in the risers. One riser might be six inches and the next seven or eight. The treads also were different widths. There were no windows in the stairwells, and if there had been lights, they had been stolen or were burnt out. Thus you might have five or six floors to ascend in complete darkness, feeling your way along a concrete banister. Then when you reached the floor of the apartment you were looking for, you had to knock on the door you thought was the apartment you were looking for. It was really spooky. There were no elevators, but even if there had been, it would be unlikely that the electricity would have been working to run them. Materials for construction were relatively inexpensive, but it was hard to find what you needed, and the lumber was random thicknesses and widths. Even pressed sheets of OSB or similar material were not consistent

Ted Lozier had helped me with the reconstruction of our office in Kokomo and would eventually help me in Haiti. Ted agreed to take his wife and three young children to Romania to construct the church. I felt we should be on hand to meet the Loziers upon their arrival. When we arrived in Bucharest, we were met by a man who drove us to Alexandria, where we checked into a hotel. The hotel had no heat, and it was snowing outside. We were given forms to fill out. I'm sure the forms were illegible, as I was shivering so hard that my hands were shaking. We went to our room, and it was frigid. There was no hot water. We had two cot-sized beds. We only used one, as we needed each other to try to stay warm. We were unsuccessful! We tried putting our heads under the cover and huffing and puffing, but that didn't help much.

The next morning, we were driven to Zimnecia. I located the apartment building where the Loziers would be staying. We began climbing in the dark stairway to the fifth floor. We knocked on the door and were greeted by a four-year-old who was dressed in a snow suit with a knit hat pulled over his ears. No, he was not going out to play, he was trying to stay warm. His mother and father appeared in heavy woolen sweaters and were very gracious and hospitable to us. The kitchen was very small. The bathroom had a bathtub that was about half full of water. We learned that this was their reservoir. They did not have any running water except at about two o'clock in the morning. During the day, there was water for the lower levels but not enough water and pressure to lift it up to higher levels, and thus in the middle of the night when there was less demand for water, the pressure would build up so that it would reach the higher levels in the building. This was used for drinking, cooking, cleaning, and washing. This was where the Loziers would be living for months during the construction. This would not be a normal construction job, as every piece of lumber had to be cut to size.

We returned to our cold room in Alexandria, and after shivering again all night, we decided we would try to stop the Loziers, as I could not bring myself to have them come to these conditions with their three small children. It was 7 o'clock on Sunday morning, and they were scheduled to leave upper New York that day. We did not know if they had already left for JFK and stayed overnight closer to the airport with some friends.

The one advantage that we had was that we were six or seven hours ahead of them. We would try to postpone their coming until spring. The post office and telephone office were across the street from the hotel. The post office was closed, but the telephone office opened at eight o'clock. I had no phone number for them, so I had to call my secretary, Carol Barnes. I gave the operator enough money, plus asked if she would get me through to the States. It worked, and at about 2:00 AM Carol's time, I tried to explain the urgency of stopping the Loziers from coming. You would have to experience the conditions to fully understand it, but I explained the best that I could. Sometime between 2:00 and 3:00 AM, she was able to connect with Ted Lozier and convince him to cancel their flights and reschedule for spring.

Finally, Ted and Jenell, along with their children, Amy, Brian, and Kevin, arrived in Romania and got settled in their apartment adapting to dipping their water out of the bathtub. Ted did an excellent job building the church and stayed through the entire project. I never returned to Romania, so I only saw pictures of the finished building, but knowing Ted, I knew the work was excellent and glorified the Lord.

Chapter 16.

Living Water Project

The wilderness and the solitary place shall be glad for them; and the desert shall rejoice, and blossom as the rose. Isaiah 35:1

In the late 1980s, our TV screens were filled for months with devastating pictures and news reports of the famine that spread across Africa from Senegal and Mauritania in the west to Sudan and Kenya in the east. Pictures showed the skeletal remains of human and animals lying in the sands of the Sahara desert.

Children, adults, and entire families were dying of starvation because of several consecutive years of severe drought. Having spent twenty years in the desert city of Timbuktu, Elaine and I were touched by the conditions. After visiting our missionaries in those areas and seeing what remained of human bones in the sand-swept desert for lack of food and water, we searched our hearts and minds as to how we could help. Money began to pour into the Mission designated for "relief." We were responsible to allocate it and see that it was used wisely and in a way that we would have results that would meet needs not only for the immediate but also for the years ahead to change these conditions.

Nomadic groups lost their means of survival. They lived as herdsman in makeshift tents. Their animals died or were slaughtered because the wells were dry and there was no grass. When there was no more food for their animals, they began to die, and soon children began dying as nursing mothers' milk also dried up.

One idea was to provide "food for work," and a plan was devised to provide wells and gardens around the water supply. The idea was to invite

Nomads who had moved into Timbuktu to receive airlifted foreign aid to plant gardens around these wells. A cone well is a large hole about one hundred feet across and about seventy-five feet deep that you can walk down into. The water table in the area was only about fifty feet. The entire cone would be ringed with gardens. The question was, will the Nomads who have never grown gardens be willing to do this kind of work? A design was made and presented to various churches, and it created a lot of interest. I was scheduled to speak in a church on a Wednesday night in Connecticut. The pastor asked me to share with his people what we as a mission were doing and planning to help this terrible situation.

At the end of the service, a gentleman who was sitting in the back of the church came to me and said he thought his father would be interested in what we were proposing. He said, "My father is presently in Italy and from Italy he is going to Australia, but he will be home in about three weeks. Would you call him when he gets home?" He gave me his father's phone number and indicated that he lived in North Carolina. So after three weeks, I called his father, and he was anticipating my call. We discussed the project that we were proposing, and I suggested that he go with me to Africa and view the area that was our interest.

He suggested that we take one of his sons. (Later I learned that he had twelve sons and four daughters. sixteen children were single births from one wife.) He indicated that his son lived in Illinois and his name was Nick. I suggested that perhaps I could visit Nick and share with him what to expect in Africa.

Elaine and I were attending the annual Conference of the General Association of Regular Baptist Churches, which that year was held in Springfield, Illinois. The schedule was open on Wednesday afternoon, so I called Nick to see if Elaine and I could drive up and visit with him. His answer was, "Don't drive up. I'll send my plane down and pick you up." Wow, this was a first! We were met at a small airport by Nick, and he drove us to his business. I guess he was in his late 20s. En route he shared with us that God had blessed him and gave him the ability to make money, so the money did not belong to him but it belonged to God. He was only the steward of what God had entrusted to him. He went on to say that his father had decided not to go to Africa but that he had a couple of brothers who would like to go.

We made arrangements that in a week or so he would pick me up at a small airport in Indianapolis and take me to Cincinnati to meet a couple other brothers who wanted to go to Africa, along with a partner of one of the brothers. We landed at Cincinnati airport, where I met with brothers John and Arie and Ron Pierre, a partner in business with John.

We arrived in Bamako on Saturday afternoon and spent the next night at the Gospel Missionary Union guest facilities. We were met there by Bob Cowley, a pilot and missionary with Evangelical Baptist Missions. Bob would be taking us on the rest of the trip.

We took off on Monday morning. After a couple hours, we needed to make a refueling stop in Mopti. As we landed, it started to pour down rain. Here I was taking these men to show them the results of the drought. It was raining so hard it was impossible to refuel, so we were obligated to stay overnight. There was a small hotel near the airport, and somehow we managed to get to it, but not without wading through nearly two feet of flood water.

The next day we made it to Timbuktu and were met and welcomed by Harold and Jean Beckley. They gave us a very *warm* reception in the baking heat. We would spend the next several days wishing for some of the rain we experienced in Mopti. Harold took us about five kilometers south of the town, where he showed us land that the governor said we could use for an agriculture project. The project site was just a sixty-acre of desert dunes with a couple of trees, thistle grass called "crum-crums," and some wicked thorn bushes.

We all slept outside under the stars in Timbuktu. It is too hot to sleep inside the house.

About the second night, I came down with malaria and began to shiver and then sweat profusely and then shiver alternately. Our beds were all lined up on a terrace, and above our heads was the bathroom window. While I was soaking my sheets with sweat, I could hear John puking in the bathroom. Poor guy was sick as a dog. We tried to give him medicine, but he apparently was never able to swallow a pill—never. At Mopti, the mosquitoes sounded like airplanes taking off from an aircraft carrier, but John could not handle a quinine pill, even camouflaged in jelly. So the night went. Some of the guys managed to sleep through it all.

I began listening to these men discussing what they wanted to do, and it all sounded great, but expensive. I was concerned about the financing of a long-term project. It has never been my temperament to ask people for money, but I knew we did not want to start something that would shortly dry up. I got the courage to stick my neck out, and I said to them, "What commitment are you men making to this project?" The answer was quick and decisive. They each committed themselves to $1,000 per month, plus they would put some "seed money" to get the project going. They also said they would give a year's notice if they wanted to withdraw from the project. Wow, what a commitment, and they have kept their word and gone far beyond!

They decided that this was their commitment and decided to go to Israel to find out how to grow plants in the desert. We left Timbuktu in the afternoon for Bamako. On the runway was a C130 cargo plane that had just delivered a load of relief foods, and the MAF plane was there, along with our EBM plane. All three aircraft would take off within minutes of each other, all headed for Bamako. The C130 was first and then MAF and finally ours. Two of our men went in the MAF plane, which would have to stop in Mopti to refuel. Nick and Arie, along with myself, flew in our Cessna with Bob Cowley as our pilot. Both Nick and Arie were also pilots, so I felt pretty safe with three pilots on board our little six- or seven-seat plane. After about an hour and a half in flight, we flew right into a terrible storm. I was in the backseat, and alongside me were two one-gallon cans of engine oil. All of a sudden I felt my seat drop from beneath me, with my seatbelt holding me to it, and the two cans of oil were airborne about level with my face. Then the pilot looked scared, as we were like a kite in the air when the string breaks, and all of a sudden our altitude went from ten thousand feet that we had been cruising at and we were sucked up to eighteen thousand feet Involuntarily, unable to bring the plane under control. Lightning flashed across the wings as we bounced from side to side and up and down. It knocked out one of the instruments. There was a door next to me, and by now I was sick as a dog and thinking we were all going to die. I was contemplating jumping out and ending my misery. The other problem everyone was concerned about was the oxygen level, as we did not have any oxygen on board, and we were at a very high, dangerous altitude point. Only God and the Cessna Company kept this little piece of machinery together. The MAF plane landed just before we did and had missed the storm by refueling in Mopti, but they said as we emerged from our plane that we looked like five white ghosts.

Richard Marshall, my nephew, and Lee Abuhl and their wives, Anna and Violet, who are Sisters, were in language study in France. They expressed a desire before going to the mission field to work together in ministering to the nomadic Tuareg tribes in northern Mali. Since most Tuaregs who survived the famine had migrated to Timbuktu or areas accessible to relief organizations, we suggested the opportunity to be involved with these same people at a location about five miles south of Timbuktu and develop the "Living Water Project." They agreed to do it.

On our arrival back in Paris, the men began immediately to contact people they knew in Israel who were involved in agriculture. On their advice, it was decided not to go to Israel but to go to Holland, where there were businesses who specialized in manufacturing equipment designed for desert conditions. I then contacted Rich and Lee and invited them to visit the men who would be the primary supporters of the project and to accompany us to Holland where we would see what was available. In Holland, we viewed some training films in the use of drip irrigation and also saw some displays of various pumping systems for pumping water, including wind and solar equipment. Arriving back in Paris, we had a day before our flight back to the United States, so the guys went to visit the Louvre, and I went to investigate fencing, as I knew our entire project would have to be fenced in to keep animals out as goats, sheep, donkeys, horses, and camels. They would eye the project like a dish of ice cream in the heat of the desert. On my way back to the hotel where we were staying, I purchased a couple kilos of grapes that I thought the guys would like to munch on since supper in France would be at least eight o'clock and maybe later. It was summertime in Paris and stayed light until after 10:00 PM and was light again around 4:00 AM.

Can you believe what happened? I watched in amazement as the guys were standing on the balcony of our fifth floor room picking grapes from the stems or whatever they are called, trying to see how many heads of people they could hit who were driving on the street below with their sunroofs open. I then realized I was traveling with a bunch of boys who liked to have fun and were full of pranks. That night I had my first taste of snails for supper. We had lived in France for a year in 1951–52, but they would have been too much of a delicacy to be served in our boarding house.

Back home, the Lord continued to provide relief. On my next trip to Mali, I was accompanied by a well driller from Minnesota. We needed expert counsel on well drilling. In Timbuktu, we found that a French company who were well drillers had set up a base and had a lot of very heavy duty trucks and well-drilling equipment. All of their equipment was manufactured in Italy and appeared to be new. They were under contract to put wells in the desert. We eventually negotiated with them to drill two deep wells on the Living Water property.

The team of Rich Marshall and Lee Abuhl had arrived in Timbuktu with their families and had begun hiring nomadic men to begin digging a cone well and a hand-dug cement well. They also had men making mud bricks for future construction of a building in which to store equipment.

At the next EBM board meeting, I requested permission to take a three-month leave of absence from my responsibilities as the general director of the mission so that Elaine and I could go to Mali to help start the Living Water Project. The board graciously granted our request. Before leaving, we began assembling a bit of equipment, including six large windmills complete with pumps and towers, hundreds of buckets, and metal cattle fencing, along with hundreds of steel post, barbed wire, a welding machine combination generator, and tools. We assembled a team of men, mostly from Bible Baptist Church in Kokomo, who would meet us in Mali in January. Elaine and I had arrived in Mali the middle of December and drove down to Cote d'Ivoire to check on the container at the port of Abidjan and have it shipped north to Mali.

Elaine and I left Bouake, Ivory Coast, on Christmas day—again as has been the case so many times in my life, it was a noteworthy Christmas—to return to Mali. When we arrived at the Mali border, soldiers met us with rifles pointed at us, and we were ordered to halt! We discovered that the day before Christmas a small aircraft entered Mali airspace from Burkina Faso (Upper Volta) and dropped a bomb (their only bomb!) on the city of Sikasso, and thus the border was closed. Sikasso was the first major city in Mali coming from Cote d'Ivoire and was close to where Mali, Burkina Faso, and Cote d'Ivoire intersected.

Now what? We could not continue, so we returned to Bouake to the Ivory Coast Academy where my brother Frank, along with his wife, Eleanor were serving as dormitory parents for high school boys. Leaving Elaine there, I flew to Bamako and arranged for a meeting with the head of the security at the gendarmerie and explained my problem. He was very sympathetic to me and told me I would be permitted to cross the border with our vehicle. I asked for something in writing. but he said within the hour the border police would be advised that we were permitted to cross. I took the next flight back to Bouake, and Elaine and I began once again to head for the border. On arrival several hours later, the police simply said, "We've been expecting you. You may pass." Thank you Lord!

Again God was so good, and within hours the tractor trailer was positioned along the edge of the river, and we negotiated with a "piroguer" (owner of a large motorized canoe) to transport the contents to Koriome.

We picked up about a dozen laborers, who began unloading thirty tons from our forty-foot container. They carried hundreds of items down the river bank and into the long, sleek handmade pirogue. We kept separate some sleeping bags that Don Marshall, one of the missionaries, had asked us to bring him.

The Kokomo team arrived around New Year's Day in Bamako, and we left the next day, with three of us crowded in the front seat and five in the back of the truck on top of all the luggage and baggage and food for the trip. We were loaded to capacity. Our destination would be Mopti the first day about five hundred kilometers north. We arrived safely after a brief stop in San to visit our former deacon and retired army sergeant who was a charter member of the Timbuktu Baptist Church. His name was Amingoin Tessegue, a godly man who was a real witness in the military outpost in Timbuktu. In San there was a small restaurant where we refreshed ourselves with some cold soda or pop, whichever, and a sandwich. We had already passed the halfway mark, and it was good for everyone to stretch their legs and get some relief for their sore bottoms. We finally arrived in Mopti at about 5:00 or 6:00 PM and pulled the pickup in front of our container. Everyone relaxed a bit, looking over this busy town where the Bani and Niger Rivers intersected. It was also a town that was infested with mosquitoes that sang in your ears and loved to bite. Besides your ears humming, your nose enjoyed the smell of dried fish, as the Bozo fishermen would bring tons of dried fish that would be marketed in the south to Burkina Faso and Cote d'Ivoire. These fish were flavored with maggots and made tasty flavored sauce in their rice and millet meals. Most maggots fell into the open fires as the cook would take two dried fish and knock them together to dislodge them.

Mopti is, in my estimation, the most interesting town in Mali. It is also an intersection of many tribal people, each with their own language and customs, and where many people speak four or five languages. This commercial town is populated with Bozos (predominately fisherman who fish along the river) Bambaras, Songhai, Bobos mostly involved with buying and selling), Bellas (laborers), Pheuls (shepherds), Dogons, and many others, just to mention a few, all with their own language distinct from the others.

We were too cheap to stay in the mosquito-infested hotel and decided to use Don Marshall's (my nephew) sleeping bags and sleep in the container. Elaine would try to sleep on the seat of the pick-up. The sleeping bags were made out of nylon, which was kind of slippery. We lined up with our feet at the lower side of the container; remember our feet would be about thirty degrees lower than our heads on our shiny hardwood floor. The rest of the story is simple; we did not sleep but spent the night sliding to the lower side of the container. At daybreak, we loaded up and were on our way. After about 150 miles, we left the road and headed north over sand tracks that we hoped would lead us to Gourma Rharous about another 150 miles straight north.

The trip was very rough, especially on the guys in the back. About ten miles south of Gourma Rharous, we came across the remains of a large French news helicopter, which crashed just a few days earlier as it was filming the Paris-Dakar Rally, an annual event when hundreds of vehicles and motorcycles race across the Sahara desert, starting in Paris and going through some of the most challenging land on earth. They traverse France, Algeria, Niger, Mali, Mauritania, and Senegal. All of the occupants of the copter were killed when it crashed into a sand dune and burst into flames. The bodies had been removed, but the guys did salvage some parts of instruments that survived the accident.

Upon our arrival at Gourma Rharous, it was refreshing to see the Niger River. Gourma Rharous is on top of a huge sand dune from which you can see for miles in any direction and especially the river as it spreads about a mile wide. Now our problem was, where was the ferry? I sent someone in a canoe across the river to summon the man in charge of the ferry. It was 6:00 or 7:00 PM when we arrived on the other side with another 150 kilometers of deep sand to get to Timbuktu. I paid the man in charge of the ferry and gave him a sizeable tip besides, as it was after normal hours when he came to get us. Everyone was tired and worn out, but we opted to continue on our way. But now there was a lot of moaning and groaning, as the guys in back were hurting. You would have to experience it to appreciate or understand it. My pen cannot express the feeling of the sore aches and pains those brave guys felt, but we were determined to make Timbuktu or bust.

It was about 2:00 AM when we finally arrived at the mission station and were greeted by Harold and Jean Beckley, and later the Marshalls and Abuhls, who were living in rented mud houses on the opposite side of the town. Somehow we all found beds that were level and fairly comfortable for our aching bodies. We made it! I am sure we all snored, but none of us heard it. It was music to our ears.

After a great breakfast and a devotional time of praise to the Lord, we met the Marshalls and Abuhls and went to the project site. A cone well was started, but due to a cave-in, which almost cost the life of one of the workers, this was halted and a traditional well was under construction.

After looking over the barren land, we continued on to Koriome. Would our big pirogue be there with our thirty tons of equipment needed to keep all of us busy for the next couple of weeks? To our delight, it had arrived during the night. We now had to unload it from the boat and load it into trucks to transport it to the project. The pirogue was about fifteen feet away from dry land because it had been loaded to capacity and had a draft of about three feet. Of course, as we lightened it by transferring the weight into the pick-ups and a large Berliet blue truck, the distance to the boat became shorter. We made several trips between Koriome and the property until all the materials were deposited neatly on the ground. A large thorn corral was placed around everything to hinder thieves from helping themselves during the night. While the people are very religious, stealing is permitted, but frowned upon if you get caught.

The next day with the use of a transit, we marked out the corners of the rectangular plot of land, which we did not own, but which the governor permitted us to use. We hoped the next appointment of a governor would respect his predecessor's generosity of giving us a drop in the bucket of the great Sahara sands. All of them have to this day.

A post driver was fabricated with the welding machine, and lines were strung with baling twine from corner to corner. This was the straightest line and looked great. There were hundreds of steel posts each with a metal arrow-like plate welded to them to give them more stability (or to show which end goes into the ground—ha!). Then the fencing was attached and stretched tight and fastened to the post. After that, a strand of barbed wire was strung across the tops of the poles. While this was going on, a mud storage building was being constructed to house valuable equipment. The team worked feverishly for two weeks making friends with nationals with whom they could not verbally communicate but with whom they demonstrated love and concern for their plight in the famine-stricken land where Christ was their greatest hope and where the materials they worked with and the food they were provided was given by Christians who shared their love and concern from thousands of miles away.

The project has continued for over twenty years. Local officials in Timbuktu identified sixty-eight families to be involved in the program. They walk to the project from their villages each day to tend to their gardens. Families keep or sell what they grow. Rows of trees were planted between the plots and around the property boundaries to provide shade and break the incessant drying wind. Leaves from the trees add organic matter to the soil. When trees needed pruning, they use larger branches for valuable fuel wood. The smaller stems and leaves are fed to their animals. Unlike large irrigation projects, which spray water into the air or transport it in inefficient canals, the water here is used efficiently. Water is pumped into reservoirs, lined with plastic to prevent seepage and with trees planted around them to reduce evaporation. The people carry water from reservoirs in buckets or siphoned through garden hoses and applied directly to the plants. The plants are planted in depressions so that the water soaks into the soil near the roots rather than running off. The people choose their own crops. During the course of a year, project families grow almost every conceivable vegetable. The list includes: okra, onions, peanuts, potatoes, melons, cabbage, lettuce, carrots, cauliflower, sweet potatoes, yams, African beans, green beans, and tomatoes. Project participants are learning how to plant, care for, and harvest many crops with which they had no previous experience. They are also learning about composting techniques using leaves from harvested plants and goat manure.

Over the years, Rich and Anna have been attacked on two occasions and robbed of equipment, vehicles, and fuel. In one attack, they were held at gunpoint, had vehicles and fuel stolen, and had their staff kidnapped. But they still continue to serve God and Tuareg people. In May 2010, they were warned by the U. S. government to leave the area because they were on an Al Qaida "hit list." It is not known whether this is because they are Christians or Americans or both! Al Qaida has moved training activities to this region, and in fact, there is a small contingent of special troops in Timbuktu to keep an eye on things. However, before evacuating, Rich was able to lead a crippled man who earns his living as a welder to the Lord. God gives blessing even when the days are dark.

Chapter 17.

"Retirement" and Reflections

And he said unto me, My grace is sufficient for thee: for my strength is made perfect in weakness. Most gladly therefore will I rather glory in my infirmities, that the power of Christ may rest upon me. II Corinthians 12:9

At age sixty-three I determined that I would retire on my sixty-fifth birthday as the general director of Evangelical Baptist Missions. About five months prior to my retirement, I was approached by this same group of Christian businessmen and benefactors that I had met in Romania and who funded the Living Water Project. Eight men were VanWingerdens; one was a brother-in-law, and again Ron Pierre was there, a partner.

The father of the VanWingerden brothers had begun a project in Haiti but was no longer able to travel, so he turned over the project to some of his sixteen children. They knew about my impending retirement, and they came to Kokomo to ask if I would administrate their project called Double Harvest—Haiti. It was agreed that we would bring Double Harvest under the umbrella of EBM and that the finances of Double Harvest would go through EBM for receipting purposes. In effect, I became the administrator (director) of Double Harvest as well as the director of EBM for several months until my retirement on March 14, 1993. At my retirement, the board of EBM asked that I stay on staff as the director of projects, which involved the Living Water Project in Mali, the Romania projects, and Double Harvest—Haiti.

Double Harvest—Haiti

Elaine and I sold our home in Kokomo and moved to central Florida. This home became our base of operations for the next thirteen years. Half of our time was spent in Haiti and half in Florida. The half in Florida was not always at home. Rather, much of our time was spent in Miami, where I purchased building materials and supplies, which were then shipped in forty-foot containers to Port au Prince, the capital of Haiti.

In Haiti, Double Harvest owned about two hundred acres of farmland, of which 150 were cultivated. The remainder housed a couple acres of greenhouses for growing flowers and ornamental house plants and where trees were planted in plugs for reforestation projects. The tree plantation had a capacity of two million seedlings per year. Three homes and an office complex with an apartment and guest rooms had been built for expatriate employees and others.

Elaine and I spent our first three months of retirement in Haiti. We hired Kevin and Rebecca Lippy to supervise the farm part of Double Harvest. Kevin was also responsible for maintenance of the farm equipment and electric generators. Becca served as bookkeeper and also taught their three children. Both Kevin and Becca had spent some time in Haiti before they were married. We discovered that years before as a little girl Becca had sailed to Africa on a freighter with her parents who were missionaries with Wycliffe Bible Translators, and we were on the same ship and even had pictures of her on the ship!

We constructed a building that was fifty feet by one hundred feet. The building was divided on the ground floor with three offices, a tool room, and a restroom, and on the second floor, there were two efficiency apartments and two guest rooms, each with a bath and three beds. The old office became guest rooms, and we were able to accommodate up to twenty in work teams. For the next few years, we would constantly have construction projects underway.

One of my responsibilities was to develop the spiritual ministry. The Lord led us to an older pastor who lived about five miles away. He agreed to come six days a week and have a devotional time with the employees of DH and also an evangelistic/devotional time at our clinic for the employees and patients. Devotions for the farm workers began each morning at 6:40 until 7:00 AM. The attendance averaged between sixty to seventy-five at the farm and ten to fifteen at the clinic. Pastor Tilus was faithful and was always about ten minutes early. He came on his horse and often had a lay preacher with him. We had a shed at the entrance of DH where we met each morning. The devotional time consisted of singing a hymn, prayer, and a message. There were several men who trusted Christ through this ministry. Pastor Tilus became ill and was unable to continue his ministry, but he sent his son, who was a seminary graduate. He continued in his father's stead. One morning prior to going up to devotions, the Lord burdened my heart to ask Lemaitre (Pastor's Tilus' son) if he would be interested in starting a church. I shared this with Elaine, and she encouraged me to approach him. After the devotional time, I approached him and simply said, "Pastor, would you have any interest in starting a church here at DH?" He immediately responded with a big smile and said, "Mr. Dave, I was going to ask you the same thing, as God has laid this on my heart."

Double Harvest is surrounded by villages with hundreds of people, many who practiced voodoo. There certainly was a need for a Christian church. Our clinic was located on the far corner of the farm, and it was decided that we would meet at the shelter at the clinic. During the week, this shelter was the "waiting room," so it was covered and already had benches. We began the next Sunday. Pastor Lemaitre brought a few people from his father's church, which included a young man who was a soloist. As in any new church, we struggled that first year, with between five and twenty attending. Around the corner from the covered pavilion the pastor's wife met with the children for Sunday school. On the second Sunday, the pastor's wife gave birth to their first child. The baby was born early in the morning, and Pastor Lemaitre walked the five miles to church after the birth and arrived on time to conduct the service. They were a committed couple. One week later, both pastor and his wife had walked to church carrying the baby.

During that first year, the Double Harvest board gave me permission to begin a trade school, which would begin with kindergarten and first grade. On another corner of the property, which was vacant, I cleared with the help of the village people what looked like a jungle. The first set of three classrooms would be in a line. Each room would be twenty feet by thirty feet to accommodate thirty students each. The second set of classrooms was built twenty-five feet parallel to the first three classrooms and bridged between to make an auditorium, which also served as a church auditorium accommodating about two hundred people. The students would be chosen from the surrounding villages. We would operate the school by seeking "sponsors" from outside of Haiti. The parents of the children would also be required to pay a very small amount in order for them to take seriously the opportunity for their children to attend school. We would need sixty sponsors at $20 per month. This would cover the salaries of our teachers for kindergarten and first grade, plus provide a hot meal each school day for the students.

We trusted the Lord to provide for this need, and He did exceedingly above what we anticipated. When school started in September, the Lord had given us ninety sponsors, making it necessary to start with two kindergarten classes and one first grade, with a total of ninety children. We had already established a rule that we would not have more than thirty students in a classroom. Most schools in Haiti had fifty to ninety students in a class with one teacher. When school began the first Monday in September, our three classrooms were already full to capacity. With the completion of the classrooms, we moved the church services to the school building. The pastor was also the director of the school, and his wife taught the first grade. Our doctor's wife was also a trained teacher for primary school, and she taught kindergarten along with another Christian teacher. Another distinctive of the school was that all grades would be taught in French. Other schools in Haiti were taught in Creole through fifth grade. All of the students were already Creole speakers, but none were French speakers. Both French and Creole are official languages in Haiti.

Each year a new class was added, so it kept me busy adding classrooms and equipping them with desk, blackboards, and chairs. We constructed a large dining room and kitchen to handle five hundred students, restrooms, offices, and storage space. We also built a home for the school director. Over the years, we added twenty-four classrooms, a vocational building, and other amenities, such as a basketball court and playground. The entire complex is walled in for the safety of the children and the security of the buildings and equipment. The school program now goes, thirteen years plus kindergarten and preschool—a total of fifteen years of instruction. The vocational building of seventy-five hundred square feet has a woodworking shop, a sheet metal/welding shop, a machine/mechanics shop, and electrical area. This is all on the ground floor, and upstairs there is a classroom with thirteen sewing machines, a drafting and technical classroom, a large kitchen and dining area for home economics classes, and an additional classroom. In another area, there is a computer classroom with about twenty computers and a library.

God very graciously gave us teams of qualified builders, plumbers, painters, masons, electricians, and laborers who worked long hours. Some came for a week and others as long as three weeks. A few came for a couple of months. These people paid their own way and gave to the Lord their vacation time. We provided the housing, but they provided their food and brought their own cooks. The amazing thing is that many of the teams came back year after year and were excited and enthusiastic. I never kept track of how many people contributed their time at Double Harvest, but without any exaggeration, there have been hundreds and maybe as many as a thousand. These worked alongside of a crew of Haitians, both in construction as well as in Vacation Bible Schools and other ministries. We organized a week-long Bible conference for Haitian pastors each January, with over one hundred pastors and Christian workers in attendance. We used friends and co-laborers in teaching, which included former missionaries John Clayton, Roger Bacon, Heath Bobbett, and Evan Drake, all former missionaries with EBM and fluent French speakers. More recently, Pierre Cadet, a missionary with EBM, has been involved with teaching these all-day sessions.

The facilities of the school, cafeteria, church, and the grounds are also used for retreats, camps, and other special events for churches in the area. I invited a specialized missionary organization out of Colorado Springs who used highly specialized volunteers for short term in planning and designing buildings for various missionary projects. This included architects, civil engineers, hydrologists, surveyors, and sanitation engineers, all working together. They did much of the design for our new medical/surgical facility, which replaced our old clinic. The former clinic was transformed into housing for the Haitian pastor and housing for the Haitian missionary with Source of Light Ministries.

Meanwhile back in central Florida, we helped start the Tricounty Baptist Church in an office building in Summerfield. This church now has moved to its own building in Lady Lake and has grown to about three hundred people, with four hundred in the winter as the snow birds attend.

In 2002, I requested that the board of Double Harvest find someone else to supervise the construction of the new clinic and surgical facility, as I was beginning to slow down physically. For the next six years, I stayed involved in the school and ministry aspects of the project, including teaching masonry to high school students. Finally, at the age of seventy-nine, I re-retired!

Today the clinic is open for business five days a week with a full staff of doctors and nurses, a dentist, a lab technician, and eye care. On the surgical side, our daughter, Diane Cable, has organized teams of surgeons, anesthesiologists, operating room nurses, and other surgical staff since the clinic opened. The teams consist of fifteen to twenty people. They are there for a week and work from 7:00 AM until 8:00 PM. They normally do 60 to 110 surgeries, depending on the severity of the cases. Many are very serious and complicated. This is all done by volunteers who pay their own way and use their vacation time. Diane takes three or four teams a year, and she goes additional times to see that all the supplies are on hand and things are ready for the team. The Lord used her in equipping most of the clinic with donated operating tables, hospital beds, lights, gurneys, surgical tools, medical supplies, pharmaceuticals, linens, gowns, gloves, and much more, including two new laparoscopes—in all several million of dollars in medical equipment!

Again the Lord did another miracle. On one of Diane's trips to Haiti, she was getting off the plane in Port-au-Prince and overheard a gentlemen talking in the aisle behind her asking the person in front of him if he knew of a hospital which had a good surgical facility that might be open to surgical teams coming to Haiti. She turned around and said, "Excuse me, but I overheard your question, and I'd like to invite you to come out to Double Harvest and let me show you our facilities." Now, yes, I believe in miracles. There are over two hundred passengers on a wide-body Airbus, everybody debarks, and there is a man in the aisle directly behind Diane who is a Christian and is looking for a place for surgical teams. He was the hospital administrator of the Baptist Hospital in Miami. Probably in the back of every seat on the plane if you would have looked you would find a full-page ad in the American Airlines magazine an advertisement for the Baptist Hospital in Miami. They advertise in that magazine because hundreds of people from South America and the Caribbean Islands come to the United States for medical and surgical help.

This hospital is also involved in missions and supports a doctor in the north of Haiti. He was not a surgeon but had many patients who needed surgery. Within weeks the hospital in Miami summoned Diane from Manhattan, Kansas, to lead their team to Double Harvest Clinic. Since that time, that part of Haiti continues to charter a bus to bring surgical patients to Double Harvest. Now then, that's not all. The wonderful part is that Pastor Gary witnesses to most of these patients, reads God's word to them, and prays with them. Several have trusted Christ as their Savior through his witnessing. Not only have many had ten to fifteen pound tumors removed, but some have had the burden of their sins removed too.

All of our children, David and Marilou Marshall, Sandy and Jake Schrader, and Diane and Ted Cable, have had a part in Double Harvest—Haiti. And five of our grandchildren, Tim, Eric and Scott Cable, and David Marshall III and Will Schrader, have participated on short term mission trips there.

Double Harvest played a key role of providing medical services and distributing international aid during the Haiti earthquake of 2010, which killed at least two hundred thousand people. You can see all of the wonderful work of Double Harvest at www.doubleharvest.org.

Reflections: The Lord's Legacy

My dear wife of well over sixty years has been my faithful helpmeet during these years of ministry. I could write another book about her, but I'll leave that up to her. We have often said to each other that if we had the choice of picking our careers again that we would do the same thing again, only now with the experience we would be a little smarter. From twenty-two years of missionary work in Timbuktu, twenty-one years as the general director of Evangelical Baptist Missions, and thirteen years in so-called "retirement" as administrator of Double Harvest in Haiti, God produced the lasting fruits of a Baptist church in Timbuktu, a prosperous mission organization, a Romanian church and printing ministry, a long-term agricultural relief project outside of Timbuktu, a thriving farm, surgery clinic, and church ministry in Haiti, and three wonderful children, nine grandchildren, and seven great-grand children. To God be the glory!

TO GOD BE THE GLORY

Great things He has taught us,
Great things He hath done,
And great our rejoicing thro'
Jesus, the Son.
But purer and higher and greater will be
Our wonder, our transport,
When Jesus we see.
Praise the Lord! Praise the Lord!
Let the earth hear His voice!
Praise the Lord! Praise the Lord!
Let the people rejoice.
O come to the Father through
Jesus the Son, and give him the glory—
Great things He has done!
Fanny Crosby (blind, but with great insight)

About the Authors

David Marshall Sr. served as a missionary in Timbuktu, Mali, for twenty years. He then served as director of Evangelical Baptist Missions for twenty-one years. During his tenure as director, the mission relocated and experienced tremendous growth. After retiring from his position at Evangelical Baptist Missions, David Marshall became the chief administrator for Double Harvest's agricultural project in Haiti. He served in Haiti for thirteen years. He and his wife, Elaine, now live in retirement in Blacksburg, Virginia.

Dr. Ted T. Cable is professor of park management and conservation at Kansas State University. He has authored eleven books, several book chapters, and scenic byway video scripts, and more than two hundred articles and presentations dealing with nature, birds, and environmental interpretation. Ted has worked extensively in Europe, West Africa, and Latin America, as well as throughout the United States, training park rangers and naturalists and designing parks and natural areas.